"From Cabin To College"

More "Cabin In The Woods" Adventures
by
Ed Kenerson

"From Cabin To College"
More "Cabin In The Woods" Adventures
by Ed Kenerson

Printed in the United States of America

ISBN 9781630500016

www.FreeChristianPublishing.com

TABLE OF CONTENTS

- - - - - - -

"More Early Cabin Years"

Introduction...5

The Critter Hotel...7

Building A House and A Home...11

Creepy Nights...15

The Woods...19

Garbage Day...22

Water Skiing Fun...25

Haircuts and Hamburgers...29

Friends and Enemies...33

We're Going To Be Rich!...36

A Boring Job...39

Aunt Irene...42

An Uninvited Guest ...46

A Dog-Gone Good Security System...50

Difficult Times...53

Number Eleven...56

The Hurricane...60

Design Flaws...64

The Teenage Years

The Baseball Champ and The Basketball Bully...68

Shoe Box Lane...72

Musical Fun...76

The Train To Washington...79

Predators...83

Doing What You Want...86

Faking It!...90

Guts, But No Glory!...93

Testing Things...96

A Life-Changing Youth Group ...99
The Slippery Slide...103
Fisticuffs...106
Dumb and Dumber...109
Blonde and Beautiful...112
Surprise!...115

The College Years

Campus Life...119
The "Man" With The Brown Paper Bag...123
The Sleep Out...126
Demonic Curiosity...129
Halloween Surprise...132
Bad Choices...135
Have Trumpet...Will Travel...138
Lessons In Humility...141
Flashing Lights...145
Circumstances...148
Back to College and A Choice...151
Studying, Statistics and Success...154
Roommates...158
The Blizzard...162
"It's The Truth!"...165
Beautiful, But Broken...168
Mrs. And Mrs. Salty...171
The Gift...174
Life and Death...177
The Movie Star...180
Graduation Day...183
A Look Backward and Forward...186

Introduction

This book is a follow-up to the popular **"Cabin In The Woods,"** a collection of life experiences I had when moving to a rural town in central Connecticut. We took up residence in an old, rustic cabin, which sat deep in the woods on a hillside knoll. There was no running water, no bathroom, no heat and no electricity, only a huge stone fireplace. In the years that followed, we built a sizable house around that cabin, but God's "country education" never stopped offering me some unique classes in spiritual living.

God blessed me with many fantastic learning experiences from those formative years. When I share them, people really enjoy the country settings, as well as the heart-felt lessons they bring. They stir their emotions and often bring back the memories they themselves have, when they were young and adventurous, too. This book is a follow-up to that book and is arranged as follows:

"More Early Cabin Years"
"The Teen Years"
"The College Years"

So, here's another bunch that God used to teach me about who He is and what He wanted for my life...I hope you enjoy them!

The Early Cabin Years

*Here are a few more experiences God
used to help me learn more about Him
during my formative years in Connecticut.*

"The Critter Hotel"

A Review Of How It All Started

"Hey, this is pretty neat," I thought to myself, as my eight year old feet clumped through the deep snow. I gazed at the old, rustic cabin in front of me. Dad, mom, my sister, Charlotte, and I were just here to look at it today. Dad had just purchased the cabin along with the 6 acres of land it sat upon. He wanted to show it to us, though we weren't going to move into it until after the spring thaw in a couple of months. After that, he would build our house around that cabin in the months ahead.

My Uncle Rene, mom's brother and a professional carpenter, would be coming down from Massachusetts to build it. He stayed with us for several days each week to manage the building process and spent the better part of the summer months laying bricks, cutting studs and rafters, nailing floor boards, raising walls and laying roof shingles. He was quite skilled and did an excellent job on what was supposed to be my parent's "dream house" in Connecticut. Overall, it would take a couple of years to complete everything. Eventually, we would have a beautiful house there instead of the old cabin that now stood in front of us, covered in snow and surrounded by overgrown grass and scrubs.

The cabin sat on a grassy knoll half way up a densely wooded hill in rural Connecticut. It was about as long as a two car garage and was clad with rough-cut, bark-covered pine boards on the outside. There was a large, plate-glass window in the front, with a sturdy, wooden door to its right. A huge, field-stone chimney was built on the right side of the cabin, reaching a couple of feet above the roof top. At the back of the cabin, just before the hill climbed steeply upward, there was an artesian well with an old-fashioned pump. The pump's long, iron handle had to be vigorously moved up and down in order to get water from 175 feet below ground, but the water was always cold, tasty and crystal clear.

All around the cabin were large oaks, colorful maples and various spruce trees, as well as plenty of prickly brush and weeds scattered around. The woods in front of the cabin were so densely packed we couldn't see the main road, especially when winter snows clung to the tree limbs.

I noticed that most all of the homes along the narrow country road below were usually built just along the edge of the woods. Mine, however, along with Mr. Arthur's house nearby, were the exception, for each of us had long, gravel driveways about the length of a football field.

There was also quite a thriving population around us…not people, but *animals!* Over the years we lived there, I remember seeing squirrels, mice, chipmunks, snakes, rats, weasels, raccoons, woodchucks, skunks, fox, deer and various other types of critters making their way through the dense woods. They never really bothered me much, unless the  dogs started chasing them, and that only proved a problem when they chased skunks, which I described in the first book. It took a lot of tomato juice baths for boy and dogs to eradicate that smell!

Because the cabin sat upon a small knoll in the middle a wooded hill, larger animals often wandered near the cabin, and some of the small ones would even try to live in the ground underneath it. They'd "weasel" their way underneath or chew themselves through the side boards, seeking a safe little area to build a nest for the long and snowy winter season.

Sometimes, I'd toss bits of bread to the chipmunks and try to catch them, but I never could…they were just too fast. My cats, however, had no problem catching them. We'd often find their furry, half-eaten little bodies in the weeds, along with other discarded meals such as field-mice and birds.

On this day, I continued to push through the snow and looked at our rustic home to be. I couldn't imagine how one could build a home around this ugly old cabin stuck in the woods with no one else around.

During that first summer, however, life wasn't easy for sure. We had no beds except those hard, wooden bunk beds built into the cabin walls. We'd hear all kinds of unknown sounds beneath us in the darkness of night... scratching, rustling, knawing, chirping and sometimes growling. If the full moon was out at night, its eerie light would slip through the clouds and into the cabin through a small window on its side. Everyone was sleeping nearby, of course, but my 4th grade mind had plenty of scary dreams from all those weird noises.

Waking up in the morning often meant hearing bacon sizzling. Mom didn't have a stove, so most often she'd set an old frying pan on a log in the fireplace. For big meals, she'd cook things on a small, propane-fueled camping stove, but either way it smelled great!

As it turned out, there was no heat until fall. The fire in the fire place kept out most of the cold, though you still shivered in the cool chill of the morning air. Again, the bathroom was just a small area off in the woods about 50 feet away, having a wooden box with a hole chiseled into it. Of course, it was fairly private, but not very comfortable. You sure didn't want to slide around while you sat on it...*those slivers really hurt!*

As I looked at the old cabin, the snow laden trees, and the solitary wintery scene all around me, I wondered what lay ahead. But, my parents reassured me, knowing that God would be with our family in this new country adventure...*and I began to get excited!*

Life Lessons

How do you face new experiences, particularly when they require significant changes? Do you believe that God cares, and that he's there to help you make good decisions? Even when you sometimes don't make the best decisions, do you realize that he's there to forgive and get you back on track?

I've found that I don't always make the best decisions. In the past I've chosen to hang with some kids I shouldn't have, and I've sometimes decided to do things that would definitely not please the Lord Jesus. But, just because I made some mistakes, mom and dad didn't kick me out of the family! That's because I was born into my family…and that can't ever change. Even kids that have been adopted are there by the *special choice* of two loving parents, who have *welcomed* a child into their family *to stay.*

It's the same with God. If you've asked Christ into your life as Savior and Lord, rest assured that in your life choices and experiences, God is there to stay and guide you along the way.

> *"But, as many as received Him, to them He gave the right to become children of God, even to those who believe in His Name."* (John 1:12)
>
> *"If we confess our sins, He is faithful and righteous to forgive us our sins and to cleanse us from all unrighteousness." (I John 1:9)*

Perhaps you've got a new, life-changing, "cabin" experience coming your way soon. That's great! Welcome it from the hand of your loving, heavenly father and be determined to make the best of it. Some changes are difficult and painful, while others are easy and enjoyable. In either case, just "faith it through," and welcome the Lord Jesus into every area of your life…you'll never regret it.

Building A House And A Home

We moved into the cabin in the spring, after Charlotte and I had just finished the school year. Uncle Rene, our carpenter and builder, hadn't yet come down to begin the building process, so we were living "in the rough," as mom and dad often reminded us (when we started complaining). The snow had gone,  but the morning air was crisp and very cool. Still, the daytime temperatures often reached into the 60's.

Cabin life was rustic! We had some electricity within a few weeks, but heat would not be ready until the fall, after the main structure of the house was completed at the end of the summer. Again, we cooked food in the large fireplace and took "sponge baths" in the mornings for weeks, until the plumbing was eventually installed.

When that finally happened, a temporary shower was set up outside the cabin in the back corner. Each of us showered there, while standing on an old piece of water-logged plywood, resting on the dirt. The shower stall was carved into the sloping dirt embankment in back of the cabin, at the beginning of the hill.

On one very hot summer afternoon, mom took a picture of me taking a shower back there after helping Uncle Rene with some cleanup chores. Over the years, she would bring out that picture, thinking it was "cute," as she put it. I was simply embarrassed to no end every time she did so. Gosh....can't a young guy have some privacy...*for crying out loud!*

Once the building process got under way, Uncle Rene would often bring his son, Roland, my cousin, along with him. That first summer found us having a blast roaming the woods, chasing squirrels, climbing trees and playing in the mud ponds formed around the newly dug, but still exposed foundations on either side of the cabin. Our homemade boat wars in those mud ponds, as I mentioned in the first book, were notorious. We were, of course, occasionally asked to help nail down the floor boards, haul cement blocks or shingles, and cart off various junk pieces of wood. But, for the most part, we just had fun!

About that time, I recall taking a walk through the woods with my new friend, John. As I mentioned in the first book, we'd make plaster molds of various animals and birds, which walked along the sandy stream beds. On this particular day, it wasn't very sunny out, and the woods were somewhat dark and foreboding. I remember seeing a small clearing in one area of the woods near his house, which had a fairly large dip in the leaf-covered ground. I wandered over to it, but as I stepped forward to see what it was, John shouted at me.

"Hey...what are you doin'?"

"Nothing, I don't think ....why?" I returned.

"You step there and you won't be going home tonight!"

He proceeded to explain that there, buried beneath all that dirt, rotting branches and dried leaves, was an old bauxite mine shaft. It had been closed down for years, and they simply stuffed the top of it with lots of old tree stumps, rotten logs and dirt. But, underneath was a 200'shaft going straight down to disaster!

"Well....it should hold me, I guess. They covered it over, right?" I was new to the woods and didn't realize the dangers that sometimes presented themselves. I was also short on *common sense.*

John scowled. "Maybe...but you go first, okay?" He wasn't really asking me to do it, just mockingly suggesting that only a fool would try it. I was already partly standing on it, but I quickly came to my senses and jumped back. I was always up for adventure, but this opened my eyes about real dangers that lay all around us at times....even when taking a slow walk through the quiet woods of Connecticut.

Life Lessons

Common sense is not always common, is it? We all have rough edges to smooth over in our lives, which means we're forever learning about what is right or wrong, as well as what is better and best. It's called discernment, and it's not as prevalent as some would have us believe. An eight year old boy walking through the woods above had no previous reference point to use as a guide for avoiding danger. My friend, John, gave me one, either to accept or reject. I thank God that I accepted his wisdom, or I might have had an *extreme* life-changing event (and I wouldn't be writing this book).

Seek to be a discerning person in your life choices at school, college and at work. You'll need a reference point, however, and for the believer, that's God's Word, the Bible. It's reliable and trustworthy, because the Lord Jesus, the author of our lives, gave it to us.

> *"All Scripture is inspired of God and profitable for teaching, for reproof, for correction, for training in righteousness, so the man of God may be adequate, equipped for every good work."* (II Timothy 3:16, 17)

Today's world is changing quickly, with advances in communications, social media, and technology. Unfortunately, moral values are quickly shifting away from the reliable Christian values upon which our country was founded. Part of this spiritual erosion is due to a lack of discernment on the part of government, education and media personalities. But, again, these folks, though sometimes helpful and correct, *are not our reference point*. The  *unchanging* principles of God's Word are what all of us must unashamedly build upon for establishing our *moral compass*, now more than ever. Following it will give you more than simple common sense. It will provide you with powerful and proven principles from Almighty God to guide you along the many trails of life.

Remember, making a wise choice to avoid stepping upon a covered-over mine shaft kept me from physical harm. A wrong choice there could have been disastrous. But, failing to discern God's will is a critical, spiritual mistake, which can lead to an eternal fall into endless suffering and *spiritual loss*. So, how's your ***spiritual*** common sense these days?

"Creepy Nights"

"Gosh...what was that?" I was nervous and talking to myself as I tried following our dirt driveway up to the cabin. It was well after dark, and I was just dropped off from a youth event at church.

The "driveway" to the cabin was nothing like the name implied. It was a couple of ruts with straggly grass growing in between those ruts and plenty of tall brush sprouting along the sides. As I mentioned before, it eventually wound its way up through dense woods before reaching a small, grassy knoll, half way up a large hill, where our cabin had been built. You can understand why folks dropped me off back at the main road. No one wanted to maneuver their car through the undergrowth or slip off the slick, stony ruts into the stream running alongside.

"Jeepers," I mumbled nervously, as I walked along, hearing strange sounds behind some trees. The stream alongside gurgled and twigs cracked as animals stepped on them in the darkness of night. The clouds were passing over the moon, so I really could see nothing more than a couple of yards ahead of me, but I still picked up the pace. I jogged around the first driveway curve and heard some leaves rustling next to my feet...and jumped. At that precise moment, an owl let out an eerie hoot to my left, and that was all I could take.

"I'm outa here!" I mumbled to myself and started running full-tilt around the bend in driveway, then climbed that slippery hill to the cabin. As I ran, I imagined the hot breathe of a ravenous bear closing in on me. A bat suddenly flew over my head and scared me even more.

"Ouch!" I stumbled momentarily on the loose stone as I reached the top of the hill and slowed to a walk. I was somewhat out of breath, but there was the cabin with its one light streaking through the trees. "Made it again," I thought to myself, relieved and happy to be home.

I remember one night, however, when I thought I *wouldn't* make it. My sister, Charlotte, had taken me to a movie called, "The Werewolf." I was fairly young at the time and was simply scared out of my mind. Later that evening I was dropped off at the beginning of the driveway at 11pm as usual from my church youth group. Again, the woods were really dark, and there was no moonlight, but a slight breeze whistled through the branches and rustled the leaves along the driveway. Every thought bombarded my brain with images of the wolf man jumping out at me from behind a tree or bush. I ran up that driveway like I was being chased by *three* werewolves, tripping over rocks and grass humps along the way. Of course, if I had just kept my eyes looking forward, instead of continually looking over my shoulder to avoid being eaten, I might not have stumbled so much. Even a few months later, after part of the new house had been built around the old cabin, I was still scurrying past dark corners in the basement and checking out closets for hidden monsters…just in case!

Later that year, we had that driveway covered with crushed stone for easier access. The hill was a different story, though, for the crushed stone on it eventually just washed away. Instead, we laid cement tracks for the car to drive on as it climbed up to where the cabin was. This made the hill easier to climb and less scary. But, in the noises of the night, I still sensed all kinds of imaginary enemies and crazed creatures ready to pounce on me. Nothing ever happened, of course, but I continued to entertain stray thoughts of impending danger throughout early years in Cheshire...especially when a nearby dog let out an eerie howl in the dark of night!

Life Lessons

Did you know that a baby is born with a fear? According to people who know about these things, at birth a baby is afraid of falling. If you look closely, when a mother gently moves a baby up and down in her arms, the baby will at times slightly jerk its little arms in the air. As a child gets older, and a parent tosses a child into the air in a fun way, the child will react less, as he or she learns to trust the parent's playful actions.

Growing up often means facing all kinds of new things we don't understand. We start obsessing over things we don't understand, like worrying about starting a new class or beginning a new job...stuff we can't totally control. More vulnerable folks worry about committing some great sin, acquiring an awful disease or being hurt or attacked by someone.

It's okay to be *aware of* possible danger, things you don't understand or situations in which you feel threatened...that's only normal and certainly not evil. The question is, "How far do we take it?"

I went to a carnival recently and entered a trailer where one paid a dollar to see the "world's largest carnivore." Inside were only three grizzly bears, though they were quite large and scary. But, I didn't run away for fear of life (though that thought may have crossed my mind!). Instead, I stood and calmly watched, from only two feet away. Why? Because there was an inch thick sheet of Plexiglas between them and me! I understood what was keeping me safe, so I wasn't unduly nervous or afraid.

Similarly, trust *God* to watch carefully over your life...to give you food, protect you in danger, lead you securely, and handle difficulties. Know that he doesn't promise us that there will be *no* pain or difficulty, just that *he will be with us* through everything and working for our good *(Rom. 8:28)*. That's fine for me, even when I don't fully understand all the details involved.

> *"Be anxious for nothing, but in everything by prayer and supplication with thanksgiving let your requests be made known to God. And the peace of God, which surpasses all comprehension, will guard your hearts and your minds in Christ Jesus."* (Phil. 4:6,7)

Hey, no matter how old your are, if a real bear is after you...run like crazy, okay! (though I hear that rolling into a ball might be a better choice). Regardless, don't bother yourself worrying about the possibility of one rummaging around in your basement, hiding in your closet or waiting in the woods to get you. Most often they're really quite content to sit quietly and eat a bunch of berries!

The Woods

Trees of all kinds surrounded the cabin, which meant plenty of colorful leaves to rake up in the fall. In the winter, some of the heavy, snow laden pine branches would actually touch the ground after a  snowstorm, bearing a foot of freshly fallen snow. After an ice storm, there would be a quarter inch of frozen rain on the branches, glistening so beautifully you knew only God could have created such beautiful handiwork.

That first summer in the cabin was a whole new world for a young boy to search out and explore. Though I would help in the building process of the new house, I had a lot of time to myself, until school started in the fall. Mr. Arthur, our elderly and well-traveled neighbor (the first book), had carved out a pathway through the woods for hiking and horseback riding. It was also fun to take off with my dog and wander for a mile through the woods.

There was also a lazy, winding stream back there, where I enjoyed catching salamanders. I'd walk along in the cool, flowing water, lifting up larger rocks quickly and grabbing one or two of those slimy, little lizard-like creatures before they scurried off to another hiding place. My pant legs were rolled up and my feet would sink into the sun-warmed sand with each step…it was great!

Salamanders were ugly little critters with four legs, webbed fingers and long tails, and resembled tiny geckos. Some were dark, some reddish-brown and others green, but all were harmless. Just trying to catch them was the most fun, though I'd let all of them go later on.

One thing I was always careful to avoid was ticks. Ticks are tiny bugs that look like miniature beetles. They would latch onto your skin and bite into you until their soft, pudgy little bodies were stuffed full of your blood about the size of a dime. Then, they'd simply fall off. Leaches the size of a string bean would do the same to you, but you would tend to feel and notice them quickly. But, ticks were easy to miss and could carry Lyme Disease, which left untreated, could cause serious health problems.

The dogs, however, were more likely to acquire these little blood-suckers. After a run in the woods with them, I'd carefully check their fur, moving it and parting it, hoping to find any ticks that had latched on. If I found one, I didn't grab onto it, for the blood-filled sack would just squish together, leaving the tiny creature still firmly attached. Instead, I'd light a match, blow it out and then quickly put it alongside the tick. Ticks hate heat and simply retract themselves in its presence.

A lot of things found homes in the woods, more than just animals. There were all kinds of plants, and lots of them grew around the cabin itself. I knew nothing about what was okay or not okay, nor did my parents. But, I found out quickly that one particular plant was a "don't touch me" plant... *poison ivy.*

If you've never had it, I truly hope you never will. Some folks, including everyone else in my family, were not susceptible to it. But, when you touch it, you get this unnoticeable substance on your hands, which causes itchy little bubbles to break out on your skin. And, it spreads like wildfire, tempting you to scratch it open, thus spreading it all the more. Gosh....it itched like crazy! I hated getting it and mostly learned to avoid the shiny, three-pointed leaves that distinguished it from other plants. But, every once in a while I'd catch it and suffer the consequences. I did find one workable solution to getting rid of it. I'd scratch it raw and then put my dad's after shave on it. The pain from dousing it with alcohol was easier to endure than that awful, unending itch!

Life Lessons

The woods can be scary to someone not familiar with them, but for me, it was just great. Still, one has to know what's okay to do, and what isn't. In the spiritual world it's no different. Some things just cause us discomfort, like poison ivy, while other things can be spiritual "blood suckers." Having discernment is critical.

For instance, there are people we know, who often bring us encouragement, support and wisdom. But, there are other people in our lives who can "infect us" like a painful tick, because they emanate ungodly attitudes and behaviors. Their way of thinking or living can even be a source of temptation to us, pushing us away from things that please God. Such a person could be a co-worker, a friend, a teacher, or even a relative. The Bible warns us to:

> "...keep your eye on those who cause dissensions and hindrances contrary to the teaching which you learned, and turn away from them. For such men are slaves, not of our Lord Christ but of their own appetites...I want you to be wise in what is good and innocent in what is evil."
> (Rom 16:17-19)

Sometimes, I wish God could have identified "good people" with a distinguishing mark on them of some sort, like a pointed head, for instance, or yellow hair. Then, of course, he might also have identified "bad people" with...say...flat heads and purple hair. On second thought, I suppose that would make life kind of boring, having just two kinds of heads and only two kinds of hair color. Then, too, I can't really think of anyone who is *all* bad or even *all* good. Bottom line? The woods are full of all kinds of animals AND people. Let's just learn how to be more discerning with whom we associate on a regular basis. Poison Ivy with plants or people spreads quickly and can really mess up your life!

Garbage Day

Living in a rural area means not having all the "bells and whistles" in community services. Take the garbage situation, for instance. There was no garbage pick-up for anyone in the entire town of Cheshire, for most of the  homes were just too scattered about. In our situation, a town garbage truck wouldn't have been able to climb the hill leading to the cabin in the summer, let alone in the snowy winter months.

So, Saturday morning each week was officially named, Garbage Day. In the beginning, we had an old trailer for that purpose, while we were adding the first wing of the house next to the cabin. That was because there was so much debris around....pieces of wood and brick, nails, tar paper, ripped shingles, paint cans and various other types of unwanted stuff. Of course, there was the normal food-type garbage, too. But, all of it filled that little trailer quite well during this first summer in the woods.

The Cheshire Dump was about 5 miles from our side of town. I don't know if you've ever had the "pleasure" of visiting such a place, but the aroma was enough to etch a perfectly *disgusting* memory in your mind. The rotting, spoiled, discarded food and chemical refuse was continually bull-dosed over and over, but in the summer time it was still especially rancid.

Now, the animal population really loved the place. I'd often pause momentarily, after emptying out our trailer, to look around at the mounds and mounds of garbage. As always, there were crows and gulls pecking at it, looking for smelly leftovers to munch on. On one side, perhaps a rat or two would scurry over the top, trying to hide from all the human activity. Raccoons could sometimes be seen, but mostly they were given to raids in the dark, even though the place was fenced in. Feral cats could easily climb the fence for a quick snack, and some of them even found undisturbed places around the outskirts of the dump to have their babies. And, if there were any bears within a couple of miles, they could certainly lumber by, break in and rummage around in the dark of night. Anyway, garbage trips were routine business on Saturday mornings.

At the cabin, the key to garbage management was keeping it separate and a good distance away from various animal raiders. In the beginning, however, we learned the hard way. We unwisely kept discarded food in garbage cans around the back of the cabin. That odor traveled and varmints came to visit us regularly for a snack. Squirrels would scratch around looking for bits and pieces to chew on, perhaps also trying to figure out how to get in. Chipmunks, weasels and skunks would hop up to the top and try to loosen the cover. But, raccoons were smart….they'd simply knock over the cans, enabling their dinner to spill out generously. For them, those early days of cabin living was often a tasty buffet!

Life Lessons

I sat down to relax and watch a television program the other day and found myself quickly turning the channel. Gratuitous sexual antics, unnecessary and bloody violence, and general "electronic garbage" filled the screen. It's hard to believe that some of the highly creative and intelligent folks in Hollywood can only come up with such refuse. Wholesome plot lines and clean action movies no longer seem to be attractive to entertainment executives, who seem interested in just increasing their profits. Television, movies, videos, books, magazines, internet, music…all these seem to be serving up spiritually spoiled food for the simple minded to indulge in. Our 21st century taste buds seem unable to enjoy the delights of a godly prepared diet. Do you agree? The Bible says:

> "...whatever is **true**, whatever is **honorable**, whatever is **right**, whatever is **pure**, whatever is **lovely**, whatever is of **good repute**, if there is any **excellence** and if anything **worthy of praise, dwell** on these things." (Phil. 4:8)

After the word praise, Paul could have added, "eat these things heartily in your spiritual diet." In other words, satisfy your spiritual appetites with what is really good for your spiritual health. Let's reverse these words in the above passage, for it gives us a picture of what is often on the *world's* menu, instead.

> "...whatever is **false**, whatever is **dishonorable**, whatever is **wrong**, whatever is **impure**, whatever is **unlovely**, whatever is of **bad repute**, if there is **lacking excellence** and if anything **unworthy** of praise, **indulge yourself**..."

Now, if you want to be a godly Christian, you don't *necessarily* have to throw away your television, never go to the movies or burn your DVD and CD collection. Mature believers simply need to make better choices in the freedoms they allow themselves.

However, there may be some whose only way of successfully dealing with all this temptation, is to literally throw away their computer or television. Yes, I know that may be extreme, but it may also be critical to their spiritual survival, because they just can't seem to keep their eyes on healthy entertainments.

Listen, if you agree that eating physical garbage is always a bad-health idea, then are you also willing to improve your *spiritual* diet today, if Jesus asks it of you? Overloading on calorie packed fats and sugars only clogs our arteries and makes us out of shape. Instead, keep your *spiritual* intake pure and godly. Doing so will keep you fit and healthy in your Christian life, and keep you in favorable standing with your spiritual Coach.

Water Skiing Fun

"Hey…watch out, Ned," shouted my cousin, Ann. "A log!"

I turned and saw the floating log just in time to slide past it in a blur. I looked ahead at Ann in the boat and waved. I didn't

shout anything back at her, because the rushing boat waves beneath me and the stinging spray of water in my face was keeping me too busy to respond.

Water skiing…it was always so much fun! On the other hand, if you hit an unnoticed piece of debris floating along the way, it probably wouldn't be fun at all. Hitting it could be quite painful, and it could send you sprawling head over heels into the turbulent wake of the boat at 30 miles per hour!

Our family took a break that first summer at the cabin and went boating with my mother's sister and family in Massachusetts. We had been busy at the cabin and needed a break, and they only lived two hours away. It was always a great weekend trip whenever we visited them.

We'd usually leave on a Saturday morning and spend the day there doing family type things. Then, on Sunday we'd leave their house real early and head to the lake trailing my cousins' boat, loaded with all kinds of paraphernalia and food.

Ann and her sister, Marcia, were more than just cousins, they were great friends. Uncle Milton and Aunt Rose got along well with mom and dad, so our visits were always great.

I remember sleeping on the living room couch in my cousins' small, cape-cod home. They had an old grandfather clock resting against the wall by the stairs, which would sound off and number its chimes every hour through the night. I'd listen to its comforting, muffled gongs and easily drift off to sleep.

"Hey....Ned....breakfast," called Dad from the guest room around the corner. Ann and Marcia would slowly slip down the stairs past me in their lounging robes and join the adults for a casual breakfast. Most everyone enjoyed eating crispy bacon and syrup-drenched waffles, but I always looked forward to my favorite entree...English muffins with cream cheese and apricot preserves spread generously on top. Along with that, a tall glass of orange juice with plenty of pulp started my day out well.

When we arrived at Long Pond lake, the dock would often be busy with weekend boaters slipping their boats into the water and rushing to "set sail" for the day's adventure. Our boat was a small 16 foot outboard with a 35 hp engine, though it struggled a bit to transport all seven of us. Once launched, we'd find a suitable spot a mile or so away along the shore to set up camp. Then, we'd start exploring the woods, swimming or skiing. Later on we'd have a great lunch roasting hot dogs and hamburgers, eating baked beans, chips and potato salad, then finishing it off with cake, watermelon and plenty of other culinary goodies.

I remember the first time that I tried to get up on water skis. With my life-jacket on, I quietly floated on top of the shallow water near the shore, keeping the tips of my skis sticking above the surface.

"Ned!" my uncle shouted from the boat thirty feet ahead, "Just hold on to the rope handle and keep your legs stiff. I'll gun it, and you should easily be able to push yourself up."

"Okay, no problem," I returned nervously.

Then, he gunned the engine and the boat surged forward, pulling me to the surface. Somehow, I accidently turned onto my stomach, which sent my skis into the air, while the boat continued to pull me along with me still clinging to the rope!

"Let go of the rope!" everyone shouted from the boat. In my confusion, I just held on and kept trying to muscle myself out of the water and onto my ski-less feet. The wake behind the boat pulled me along half-submerged, while creating a huge wave. Finally, I came to my senses and released the rope about the same time my uncle powered-down the boat. Now…that was embarrassing!

After a couple more attempts, however, I finally got up on two skis and enjoyed an uneventful ride around the lake. Eventually, I was able to slalom on one ski, hopping over the boat's wake from side to side at will. *Great fun!*

Life Lessons

Learning….it's not always an easy or fun experience. Water skiing was fun to learn, but not everything is so enjoyable the first time round. With the things of God, learning can even be an extended process with many repeat lessons (unfortunately, right?).

Think of all the things we've got to learn about God and his will for our lives…how to pray, how to read the Bible, how to share our faith, our to use our spiritual gifts….and the list goes on and on, doesn't it. So, how are you doing in this process? Is God pleased with your progress? Here are some thoughts on learning.

First, every believer has to take the life class called, "Learning to Please God 101," for no one this side of heaven is perfect. Yes, a believer's sins are forgiven and heaven awaits him or her, and nothing can change that as I understand my Bible. But, we all mess up really bad at times, and have to come humbly back to the Lord for forgiveness.

Second, there's *no* plateau where we can rest, look back and say, "Okay, I've finally arrived; it's downhill from here!" Regardless of your physical or spiritual age (when you came to Christ as Savior), the process continues. You'll still have to face temptation in the form of personal weaknesses or pleasures outside God's will. Along the way, you'll continue to learn how to trust God in the difficult times, "faithing-it-through" until God brings you home to heaven. No one is exempt.

Thirdly, the key to spiritual success is wisdom. Wisdom involves three things:

Discerning   Deciding   Doing

Let's use the example of putting a golf ball into the hole at your local miniature golf range. You search for the best angle among many (discerning), you select which shot you wish to take (deciding), and then you hit the ball (doing).

You might think that wisdom happens when you successfully put the ball in the hole...but, such is not the case. Wisdom is learning to remember and apply the principles that made you successful in the first place. So, *discern* God's will, *decide* to follow it, and then *do* it with consistency. When you <u>keep</u> doing the things you've learned, only then will you become a wise believer in your attitudes and behaviors. Proverbs 13:18 (NIV) says:

> *"He who ignores discipline comes to poverty and shame, but whoever heeds correction is honored."*

"Haircuts and Hamburgers"

It was only a quarter mile walk from the cabin through the woods to get to the barbershop....Joe's Barbershop, to be specific. Everybody knew who "Joe the barber" was in our small, rural town of Cheshire. His business was located in a small shopping plaza along the main road on the east side of the town.

Other than a few other stores around this little plaza, there wasn't much else built or being built. There was a grocery store, a Dairy Queen, a gas station, a pizza place, a Friendly's Ice Cream store and a small roadside motel. This main road, Route 10, was a two lane road cutting through the countryside connecting Hartford and New Haven, each one being about 45 minutes away from Cheshire by car at that time. Later on, major highways a few miles to the north and south easily cut the travelling time by half.

I crossed the street in front of our driveway and then made my way across a huge field of uncut, grass as high as my shoulders. A short patch of woods remained before coming to an abandoned dirt road, which I followed to route 10, by the Dairy Queen. It really wasn't more than a 15 minute walk.

"Hi, Kenerson," greeted Joe, "time to get your ears clipped again?" Joe knew everyone by name.

"Yeah, I guess," I responded, without much excitement.

"Alright, then, just take a seat…be with you shortly." I strolled over to an old wooden chair with a worn, leather insert on it. There were three others in front of me on this Saturday morning, and Joe was in the midst of a deep discussion about horses.

"Yes, I just purchased my first one....and it wasn't cheap, either, let me tell you."

The man in the chair responded. "Nope...never are."

Joe continued as he clipped along. "But, I built a small horse barn and the kids really love to help take care of it. Now, I'm not rich at all, mind you, but I figured it was a good family thing...you know."

"Yup...something they'll remember," responded the guy sitting to my right, who was next in line.

"You got it, Tom," affirmed Joe. "It's all about family. I mean, otherwise it's just a waste of money, right." Everyone nodded in agreement...I just listened. Joe was a great talker.

"On the other hand, I never realized the mess I'd have. Man, every day someone's got to clean the stuff up, know what I mean? Hey, but life's great anyway." Again, everyone seemed to just nod in agreement.

Joe paused for a moment, coughed slightly, then continued. "By the way, did ya' hear about what the President said on the TV last night about Russia?" This, however, did start up a rousing discussion for the next few minutes. Joe seemed to always have something to ask or comment on, which made my trips to his barbershop quite interesting and....well, even educational.

Soon it was my turn, and he buzzed me quickly, followed by a few clips here and there. I got up, paid him and said goodbye, thinking the lessons on equestrian care and political strategy were very interesting.

Since it was now our first fall in Connecticut, I had recently started school and made some new friends. So, I was off now to Friendly's across the street to meet my friend, Joe. The both of us loved eating there, for a Friendly's "Big Beef," cooked medium/rare with lettuce, tomato and mayonnaise, was *fantastic!* We each followed it up with an "Awful Awful," a huge, tasty milk shake made thick with your favorite ice cream...boy, was it great!

Joe lived about a mile away, so his mother dropped him off to meet me, while she shopped nearby. "Hey, why don't you come on over, when we're done?" Joe asked.

"Okay, I haven't beaten you in a game of tennis in a while, anyway."

"Right....in your dreams!"

We spent the rest of that Saturday playing tennis, basketball and watching some old westerns on TV. Joe's house sat on the corner of a quiet country road and was quite large, though old. His family had several acres of land, a fairly run-down tennis court with a couple of basketball hoops at each end, and an old, empty horse barn.

Joe's mom was great, always taking time to talk with me about the cabin house and how things were coming along. Or, she'd talk with us about school or other things interesting to us. It was great to know another adult was genuinely interested in your life.

Life Lessons

I never had much of a problem relating to adults growing up. Joe the Barber was just a nice guy, who was as interested in my life as a young boy as much as he was with his adult customers, and I liked him for that. And, my friend's mother was the same way, kind, helpful and always ready to listen to our thoughts and ideas. That made me think about how I get along with others today, who I may not know as well, or perhaps, are just different from me.

At the back door of my house, we have a mat that doesn't say anything on it. But, on the other hand, my neighbor has one that colorfully and boldly says, "Welcome." I think Christ wants us to be people who have the "Welcome" mat out in our relationships such that it's obvious to everyone we meet. Now, that's difficult at times, I know, for some folks are much easier to get along with than others. But, because God is love, we ought to be kind and patient with others, too, since we are his children of faith. When people see and talk with us, they should see and hear Jesus, no matter what age we happen to be.

> *"We know that we have come to know him if we obey his commands. The man who says, "I know him," but does not do what he commands is a liar, and the truth is not in him."*
> (I John 2:3-4 NIV)

I don't know if "Joe the barber" was a believer, but I do know that he was *like Jesus* to me at a young age, and so was my friend Joe's mom. They made life enjoyable, and I'm thankful I knew them both.

Friends and Enemies

In the first few months of the cabin experience I had to make some new friends, which didn't come easily. I don't know if you happen to make friends easily, but making friends is still an important process to do carefully for any of us.

George was older by a couple of years and lived only one house away from us up the road, a five minute walk through the woods. We played football in the fall, hockey in the winter and baseball in the summer with some of the other neighborhood kids. I believe he later became a local cop in that small town of Cheshire and had a successful career in law enforcement.

Annette was a sweet and quiet girl, who lived about an eighth of a mile up the road. I visited her from time to time, mostly just to talk, or perhaps to take a walk together. She had a large German Shepard, which nobody but the family could get near. I remember waiting at the bus stop one day, when her dog suddenly got loose and came charging after me! I ran as fast as my feet would carry me, but it latched on to my ankle. Her parents pulled it off me, but I don't remember visiting Annette too often after that experience!

As I mentioned before, one of my best friends was a fellow by the name of Joe. We often visited each other's house for the day, playing board games, competing at basketball and trekking through the woods. I was better at tennis, he was better at basketball, though each of us thought we were the best at everything...*of course!* On occasion, we camped out in the Cheshire woods or hiked up Sleeping Giant Mountain nearby. We had a lot in common and remained good friends over the years.

Then, there was Steve....another great friend. We were both part of the youth group at the Baptist church, called Cheshire Teens. So many things come to mind about my friendship with Steve, I don't know where to begin. There was the time we joined a fledgling business called Amway and tried to sell soap products to families in the church and in the town. That lasted about a week, though we thought we would become millionaires overnight! We pulled in a few bucks, but that was it.

I also recall a time later on, when we both went to camp in Colorado with a bunch of kids from our church youth group. The bus trip from Connecticut to Chicago was long and boring, but the train ride from there to Colorado was exciting. It had a "vista" car with a sight-seeing level, where one could see the countryside whisk by in all its beauty. From the Kansas grass lands to the majestic, snowed-topped Rocky Mountains, I was just in awe.

While at Silver Cliff Camp, the leaders actually brought all 100 of us half way up one of those snowy mountains stuffed together in a 50 foot trailer truck. Getting there involved easy highway travel at first, but later meant being jostled along on a pot-holed and muddy  mountain road. As we moved to higher elevations above the tree line, the temperature was much cooler...hovering around 50 degrees or so, but snow still covered the mountain landscape. They emptied us out and let us slide down the long, deep pathways they had carved out of the snow. Sliding down those paths was better than a fast ride at Disneyworld, though we did get quite wet. By the time everyone got back to camp, however, and its 80 degree weather, we were completely dried off.

Steve and I were on competitive teams all week and had a ball trying to out-do each other. We had to create a team slogan and song, a team skit and compete in daily events. I'm not sure who won most of the competition, but Steve's friendship meant a lot to me through the years.

Life Lessons

The other day I went to a fast food restaurant and ordered a hamburger at the window. Unfortunately, they forgot the drink, and I had to go back for it, but this time I went inside. Now, the original girl had an inviting attitude, but the girl from whom I went back to pick up the drink, was annoyed by the whole thing. I don't know if she didn't believe me (I had the receipt) or just didn't want to be bothered (she kept talking with her friend behind the counter about her dating life). Either way, I'd give her a "D" in customer service.

Friends are people who genuinely like you and want to get along. Christian friends are even better, in most cases, because they realize that love is more than a feeling, it's a responsibility. That's someone worth hanging around with...someone who is reliable, trustworthy and really cares.

Someone said to me that the people you get to know quickly don't necessarily qualify as friends. You may like them and have fun together, but genuine friends *prove themselves over time.* I know someone whose friend suddenly turned against him, and it hurt, for the trust element was shaken beyond repair. Other relationships can melt away due to incessant jealousy or unnecessary competition. Even a married person's trust is often shattered by a spouse's unfaithfulness...the one who was his or her close friend. So, be sure to choose your friends carefully.

By the way, friendship with God is important, too. His guideline for friendship is this: *"You are my friends if you do what I command."* (John 15:14) Are you a reliable and trustworthy friend to God? In the long run, nothing else will matter, will it?

We're Going To Be Rich!

Fall is one of my favorite seasons of the year, with its cool breezes, cloudy skies and colorful collages of fallen leaves. As we faced our first winter in the cabin, the bending trees spoke of subtle,  but unavoidable signs of impending winter cold.

It was one of those October days, when my father came home sharing some exciting news. Apparently, there was a distant family member of significant wealth living in Chicago, who had just passed away. His lawyer had researched the family name and tried to locate as many relatives as possible, one of whom was my father. The news dad shared about all this warmed us up quickly, for apparently, we might be in line for some of the financial proceeds from the man's estate.

"Are we going to be rich?" I asked excitedly.

"Probably not, Ned, but there could be enough to help us along. Frankly, I'm really not sure," was his reply.

"We won't know until we get to Chicago and find out," added Mom. "When do we have to leave, Ed?" she asked him.

I don't remember all the details after that except that we left the next week for an important appointment with the lawyer in Chicago, over a thousand miles away. The prospect of gaining some additional income to finish the cabin-to-home transformation would be a welcome change. Perhaps my parents' "dream house" could be finished right away.

The trip to Chicago took a couple of days each way, so we stayed at small, inexpensive motels along the way. The day after we arrived, we went downtown to deal with all the legal questions.

I had never been in a big city like Chicago before. Again, I was about 8 years old at the time, and my eyes couldn't even see the tops of many of those skyscrapers. The subway and streetcars were neat to ride on, but the people always seemed to be in a rush, as they crossed streets and scurried from building to building. The slower pace of country living was something I preferred, even at this young age.

Well, bottom line, we ended up *without a dime* from the estate. Apparently, there were problems in tracing the exact family tree and dad couldn't justify to the court that we were entitled to any money or possessions. So, the trip back was not a happy one, and our hopes were quite flattened by reality. Even the weather conveyed that feeling. The sunny and warm weather of the previous day had now changed to an overcast, drizzly day of intermittent showers and darkened clouds. We arrived home, and the new bills for the new house had piled up. Had my parents "bit of more than they could chew?"

Life Lesson

Why do people want to get rich? We had a lot of bills from the building of the new house and just wanted to pay those off. However, in the back of our minds was the thought….however distant…that acquiring a lot of money might bring happiness. The Bible clearly warns us about such an attitude:

> *"But those who want to get rich fall into temptation and snare and many foolish and harmful desires, which plunge men into ruin and destruction. For the love of money is a root of all sorts of evil..."* (I Tim. 6:9-10)

Money isn't evil, just the love of it. I think God is saying here that we shouldn't crave or strive to have lots and lots of it. What happens to those who do crave after it and relentlessly strive to obtain wealth is that such folks are no longer focused upon God and serving him. Instead, they begin to subtly find their central purpose or life focus in something *other* than God's will.

Remember when Satan tempted Eve in the Garden of Eden? His enticement was for them to "be like God." He was offering Eve an opportunity, falsely so, to run life on her own terms: *"Why be concerned about what God wants. Think for yourselves and do your own thing. You don't really need Him, anyway, do you?"*

We think that lots of money eliminates the need for God. We don't have to pray for food, clothing, safety, shelter, transportation, entertainment, education, vacations….anything, because we just write the check, right? But, that's not true in any sense. James reminds us that, *"You do not know what your life will be like tomorrow…instead, you ought to say, If the Lord wills, we will live and also do this or that."* (James 414, 15)

My friend, the truth is that God is in control…like it or not. Our lives *always* live in the shadow of his sovereign purposes. I might not live another second, if he chooses to call me home, regardless of the amount of material toys in my house or the financial treasure in my bank account.

My parents weren't greedy, just seeking God's leading, which perhaps could have been added income. That's fine. But, let's be careful about dreaming for materialistic things and for large amounts of greenbacks in your wallet or purse. Your future is *in heaven,* if you know Christ. Do you know him? Are you rich toward God?

A Boring Job

After a short while, my parents thought it might be good for me to find some kind of part time job, so I could learn a few things about personal responsibility. So, I got a job on Saturday mornings doing grounds-keeping work at Mr. Arthur's nearby estate.

In the first book, I mentioned that he was an elderly, retired gentleman, who lived about a half mile away…just a short walk through the woods. He always had plenty of things for me to do around his house…raking leaves in the fall, sweeping the porches, trimming the bushes, cutting the lawn….etc.

I especially remember how he'd call me over and just chat about some of his life adventures. He was well traveled and knowledgeable about history and various cultures around the world. On one occasion, he brought over his *own* book. It was a personal autobiography of his life, stuffed with pictures about the time he was in the Navy and the many high profile positions he held thereafter in life. He'd flip through it and elaborate on all the details behind each picture.

He told so many stories about the sea one could listen for hours. He talked about ships tossing in the rough, frothy swells of the ocean, as well as stopping off at foreign ports of call like Beijing or London. I enjoyed talking with him, frankly, because he'd often pull me off a job just to chat…and I enjoyed the break! Hey, when the boss doesn't mind paying you for taking some time to listen to his stories and travels, sounds pretty good, right? Actually, I think his rambling stories and enticing travels helped to shape me for doing what I like best....my own writing.

But...back to the work idea. From the first book, you already know that I didn't like raking leaves around the cabin, and there were lots of them on the ground in the fall. But, Mr. Arthur's house sat on a huge hill in the middle of the woods and was surrounded by hundreds of trees. Some of them grew individually at various places on his huge lawn. Each usually had a mound of ivy at its base or, perhaps, a small stone fence around it. Leaves would accumulate in there, and it was almost impossible to rake them out. So, let me emphasize again, *raking bored me silly!*

There were other things that drove me over the edge, too. One was painting the house, so it was also high on my list of things to avoid. There was nothing to paint in the cabin, but there was plenty to paint later on in the new house. First, you had to scrape off any layers of old paint that had bubbled up over time. Then you added a primer coat of thin white paint, which the wood could absorb deeply. Last, you'd add the final coat, hoping that one coat would cover well. Otherwise....yup...you'd even have to add a second coat!

Another bad work idea was cutting brush along our long driveway. It clearly had to be done, because each spring brought a surge of new, green scrubs along both sides, sometimes right in the middle. That was the worst. One had to bend over and pull up every unwanted, annoying little sprout pushing its way up through the dirt and gravel...all the way to the house!

Other bad work ideas were washing the cars and the dogs, taking the garbage to the dump every week, shoveling the top of the driveway after a snow storm, cleaning out the crawl space under the cabin, clearing out the gutters (first book), and de-pooing the rabbit cage. After a week, all the droppings from those two pet rabbits falling through the wire floor would be a foot thick (okay…a few inches, but it was still nasty business!)

Life Lessons

Work…I've learned the hard way that you just can't avoid it. But, let me share a positive about it and focus on the word *discipline.* Discipline has to do with *training.* In other words, what do you do, which you are not necessarily "required to do," but you do it simply because it assists you in your overall spiritual development? What well-chosen "to dos" or "not-to-dos" do you practice (work hard at) in order to *facilitate* your spiritual growth?

> *"…discipline yourself for the purpose of godliness; for bodily discipline is only of little profit, but godliness is profitable for all things…"* (I Tim. 4:7, 8)

For example, all coaches in the sports world have drilled the mindset into their athletes to delay satisfying anything which could hinder performance on game day (e.g., working out, running, etc.). Our spiritual natures react the same way. By putting off certain things, I enable my inner person to become more spiritually focused. And, by disciplining myself to do other things, I enable my inner person to grow stronger as well. Here are some examples:

1. Memorize scripture.
2. Listen to a Christian CD *every* week.
3. Read a Christian book *every* month.
4. Pray *every morning* for an opportunity to share your faith.
5. *Immediately* turn off *any* compromising TV programs.

These are just some of the things that can help you live in a way that pleases the Lord. Try them out or make some up for yourself, remembering consistency is the key to their success.

So, I guess work is here to stay. But, "work smart" and plug some spiritual disciplines into your life. Try it…it *works!*

Aunt Irene

Relatives are ours for life...one just can't order new ones. We sort of "get what we get" with our relatives, right? I mean, you can't  reorder a new set of relatives that fits more to your liking. It is what it is, and they are what they are!

Well, first let me describe Aunt Irene, my mother's sister, who was, frankly, one of those you might have considered reordering. I don't say that because she was a bad person...just that she was a bit strange. For instance, after most of the outside structure of the house had been built, she invited Irene down to visit, and Aunt Irene accepted the invitation.

My mom had ten brothers and sisters, but Irene definitely stood out from the rest. She fully believed in aliens, even believing she had seen some, perhaps even knowing some personally. She was into all the books and magazines that talked about aliens and attended conferences about them, when she could.

Aunt Irene was also very artistic, and had a small shop outside her home in New Hampshire, where she sold her paintings. She wasn't very good at it, but it made her happy, so while at our house, she decided to paint a portrait of mom. So far, so good.

A week later, however, she revealed her work to us all. Without being nasty, my reaction was this: "Are you sure that's my mom, I mean it really doesn't look like her very much?"

Aunt Irene smiled, saying, "But, this is how I see her."

I thought to myself, "Either it resembles her or it doesn't. What's the deal?"

"Ned," she lectured, "an artist paints what she feels, not just what she sees.

"Okay, let's call it a feeling, instead of a portrait. Either way, it stinks!" (No, I didn't really say that, but I felt like saying it!)

Of course, you couldn't change her mind anyway, for she always said, "It's all about an artist's *interpretation.*" I figured it this way...if a portrait really looks like a person, it's good; if it doesn't, it's not a good portrait. On the up side, I think my aunt would have made a good Zen philosopher or, perhaps, an alien photographer.

Well, my aunt's picture hung in the hallway for years, until she passed away. Strangely enough, somehow it got lost soon after that. Perhaps, it's nailed to an art-loving Martian's bedroom wall somewhere? (just kidding!)

Next, there was Uncle Lionel, who was truly a creative and inventive mind. He was always engineering home-made machines, like turning an old lawn mower into a go cart for his kids, or making an old car into a 4/4 off-road vehicle. Amazing talent.

One time, while we were still living in the cabin, we took a trip up to the relatives and stopped by his house. "Ned," he asked, "go outside, okay, and get me some pieces of colorful rock, things like quartz."

So, I went outside to retrieve some small stones as he requested. Nearby was a dirt and stone road, so I walked along the edge and garnered a handful. When I returned, he took just five of these colorful, crystal-like stones and placed them in a small container the size of a drinking glass. It was half-filled with a water and sand mixture. There was also a thin, metal rod with irregular fins on its end that went into the water, after you closed the top and secured it. Then, when you plugged this little contraption into a wall socket....like a juicer...and it would slowly churn round and round for hours. I didn't think much of it, until he showed me some stones on the table that had been "polished" in it overnight. They were now shiny, finely smoothed and brightly colored pieces of stone he would sell to jewelers throughout the area. And, he made good money doing it. What an inventive guy!

I could go on about my Uncle Jerry, a war hero, who survived captivity in a WWII, Japanese prisoner of war camp. What amazing stories he could tell.

Then, there was Uncle Donald, who was a pastor of a small Baptist church in Flagstaff, Arizona. He had a near-fatal hunting accident, which sent him to a hospital emergency room in order to save his life. While under the knife, the surgeons discovered something more serious than a stray bullet in his shoulder. His entire heart was being surrounded and strangled by a strange, fatty growth of some sort. It would have soon claimed his life, if they hadn't discovered and removed it. He continually praised God for watching over his life, and went on to have a very powerful pastoral ministry for years after his hunting "accident."

There are many other stories to tell about others in my mother's side of the family. My father's side wasn't so interesting, so nothing there to focus upon. Relatives…they come with the territory!

Life Lessons

Family is so important, both one's immediate or extended family. The family unit is designed by God to have a loving, responsible dad in the lead, with a nurturing and supportive mom alongside. Both have the responsibility to raise children to obey God's principles of life found in the Bible. Be aware that in our schools, colleges and society today, you'll find that there are some misguided folks who think that families can still be called families without them being so traditionally focused. They are dead wrong and are causing great harm in our world today.

But, in this context, I want to stress why your family relationships are so valuable. Irene was a bit different for sure, but that didn't mean that I really didn't like her or learn from her. She was very kind and thoughtful in many ways, something all of us could improve upon, right? Her husband Hank was a great conversationalist, who had a wealth of knowledge. I thoroughly enjoyed listening and learning from him. Watching Uncle Rene build the house helped me learn hundreds of practical skills that I later used on my own home. Such skills would have cost me a lot of money to hire out, but instead, I know how to do them myself. My conversations with Uncle Donald showed me his commitment to Christ, along with his sense of compassion and deep faith in the Lord. Mom and dad, of course, mostly showed me how to have a wonderful home, full of love and support.

I've said all this to reaffirm that no family is perfect. But, if you're blessed with a great family, be thankful. But, if you're not, for whatever reason, it doesn't mean you're weird or that God doesn't love you. God will fill in the gaps, as you pray to him and follow Biblical principles. Jacob had a dysfunctional family life, and Joseph was permanently kicked out of his family, but God blessed them both and used them mightily. Remember, everyone should be living out the following truth:

> *"...to put their religion into practice by caring for their own family and so repaying their parents and grandparents, for this is pleasing to God."*
> (I Timothy 5:4 NIV)

An Uninvited Guest

"Now...that will put hair on your chest!" announced my eight year old cousin, Richard. He smiled victoriously after finishing a huge plate of roast turkey, mashed potatoes and other  Thanksgiving Day goodies. He was addressing his 10 year old sister when he said it, who didn't seem very enthusiastic about the idea. Richard, however, was just repeating what his father often said when eating something really good. I thought it an odd thing to say to a girl, but at my age I didn't exactly know why.

Uncle Rene invited us up to his house to enjoy Thanksgiving together along with some other extended family members. He had built his own house in rural Massachusetts, and it was large enough to hold his family of twelve and other guests. He wasn't a wealthy man, but having 11 kids forced him to build a big house. Since the cabin transformation was coming along fine, we were glad to attend.

As I looked around the room there were 25 people eating, smiling and telling funny stories that made people laugh. The adults sat around a regular kitchen table, while all the kids sat around a makeshift table consisting of sheet covered, 4'X 8' sheet of plywood resting on two sawhorses. A sawhorse is a wooden bench standing about 3 feet high, on which carpenters cut or saw lumber, when building a house. The table was a bit shaky, but all of us kids easily fit around it.

46

There was also a huge, stone fireplace next to the table, big enough for several of us to climb in and out, if we wanted to. Built into it on the left side were two ovens in which Aunt Terry had cooked a couple of 30 pound turkeys. The house was still being worked on, so there wasn't much furniture...just a few old couches and chairs.

The floors were rough-boarded wood with scatter rugs here and there, and the walls had simple wood paneling on them. The living room area was actually quite large and had my uncle's favorite thing in it to brag about...his stereo system. He built it into the wall with all kinds of flashy lights and technology.

I got up from the table and looked briefly out the window. The day was cold and wet, with occasional snow showers carpeting the ground. I thought to myself how much fun it would be to get caught in a heavy snow storm on the way home with 4 or 5 feet of drifting, blowing snow...a genuine blizzard! I shared my idea, but no one really agreed, so I just enjoyed picturing it in my mind.

After dinner, everyone continued to tell stories to each other in little groups. Grown-ups talked in the living room, and kids played throughout the house or outside in the yard.

At one point, I walked into the bathroom to see how my uncle was building it. The tub was in the corner, held firmly in place by pieces of rusty colored field stone he had taken from the woods nearby. The floor and walls were still unfinished, but the sink and toilet worked fine. Again, his house, like our cabin home, was still a work in progress.

Suddenly, I saw something move in the corner behind the toilet. I shouted out in surprise, not loudly, but enough to catch the attention of my uncle, who happened to be walking by. He came in, saw what was lurking behind the toilet and quickly grabbed my arm. He yanked me away and behind himself, while at the same time reaching for a broom leaning against the wall. Everything was happening so fast, I really didn't know what to think.

Then, I saw a large black "something," as big as a cat. It snarled and jumped into the air toward my uncle's throat. Uncle Rene darted to the left and the animal flew right over his right shoulder. It landed with a weird screeching and hissing sound in the opposite corner.

"Get out!" he ordered, and believe me, he didn't have to say it to me twice. Reaching the door, I turned and saw my uncle slamming the wooden end of the broom into the vicious creature he had pinned to the wall. Finally, it stopped moving.

I was scared silly and had good reason to be. Uncle Rene later explained to all of us that it was an exceptionally large sewer rat. Somehow it had come up through the new plumbing line *into the toilet* and got loose in the bathroom. I was very fortunate that he had been walking by. Otherwise I might have been bitten and caught a serious disease.

Life Lessons

I didn't expect that sewer rat to be in the bathroom, and I know Uncle Rene didn't want it there, for sure! Nevertheless, it did get in there, even though he had tried to avoid that type of thing happening, when he built the plumbing system.

Unexpected troubles and spiritual incursions into our lives happen to all of us at times. It could be the sudden loss of someone you love dearly or perhaps a health-related problem causing great anxiety or pain. But, I think one of the worst kinds is having to face a sudden temptation that you're not ready to face...and win over it. Of, course, that's what temptation is all about, right? Temptation is being pressured within or without by something that draws you into it, something that stirs you with unguarded interest or immoral intent. And, if you give in, you disobey either your own conscience or God's will....or both.

> *"...each one is tempted, when by his own evil desire, he is dragged away and enticed. Then, after desire has*

conceived, it gives birth to sin and sin, when it is full-grown, gives birth to death." (James 1:14, 15 NIV)

Have you ever seen a rudder on a large ocean liner lifted out of the water for repairs? It has a huge 50 foot or larger piece of steel at the stern, which is buried underneath the water's surface. It pushes against the flow of the water to the right or left, thus redirecting the ship according to the captain's commands.

Not to over simplify things, but it is true for all of us that Christ is our spiritual captain, and we are his crew. There are many strong impulses flowing toward us, some good and some not good, but it is up to us to turn the rudder of our lives in obedience to God's commands.

In the same way, temptation always presents a choice...will I please my own driving sense of earthly and temporary pleasure, or will I please Jesus, my Lord? It can be a very difficult decision, when one is in the presence of an enticing activity, entertainment or ungodly relationship. Here are two sayings that have helped in such situations:

1. There is *nothing* more *valuable* than doing God's will.

2. Don't do what *feels* good; do what *is* good.

If you seriously take time to consider and pray over these two principles, God will use them to keep you on the "straight and narrow" pathway, even in the presence of a vicious, snarling temptation!

> *"...I count all things to be loss in view of the surpassing value of knowing Christ Jesus my Lord, for whom I have suffered the loss of all things, and count them but rubbish so that I may gain Christ."* (Phil. 3:8)

A Dog-Gone Good Security System

Dutchess, my long-haired sable collie, proved to be a great watch-dog for anyone walking up the driveway or wandering in the woods nearby. She looked like Lassie and was quite docile most of the time. But, she would bark ferociously at squirrels, raccoons and any other varmints that happened by the house.

The problem was, of course, when people stopped by. When we were nailing boards and studs in the new house, we sometimes couldn't hear a car approaching or a voice calling to us. But, any stranger coming upon the scene would not miss Dutchess's attention, and she would tear around the house to "greet" them. Now, at 70 pounds or so, she wasn't very intimidating size-wise....until she opened her mouth. Then, she could really scare or intimidate you with her barking and growling.

Though she never bit anyone, we didn't want any heart attacks either, so we built a "run" in the back of the house by the dog cage. The cage was made of strong chicken wire and was about the size of my bedroom. It also had a wooden, enclosed shelter for Dutchess (and later, Duke) to get out of the cold, rain and snow.

The actual "run" was a thick, 20 foot wire stretching from one tree to another in front of her pen...about 7 feet high. We then attached Dutchess' collar to a 10 foot chain leash and tied *it* to a moveable ring. The ring slid easily along the long wire, back and forth as the dog wanted. Sometimes she'd take off after squirrels or birds scurrying along nearby, only to find herself yanked to a fast halt, when reaching either end of the line. That was only in the beginning, of course, for she learned when and where she had to stop. Overall, my only question in building it was, "Is it safe and secure?" I wanted to know that she couldn't get hurt from it.

One fateful day, I got home from school early and was in the bedroom starting my homework. Suddenly, the quiet was interrupted by my mother shouting, "Ned...Ned...come quickly. *Dutchess is in trouble!"*

I jumped off the bed and ran through the house to the back door, where mom was now anxiously pointing to Dutchess. She wasn't barking or growling, just giving a high-pitched whine. Dutchess had wrapped herself around a small, nearby tree....how she had done so, I don't know. But, she was wound so tightly that her leash was literally choking her to death. As she pulled the chain around the tree to free herself, she only tightened the leash even *more*. Mom was beside herself, not knowing what to do, so I ran out the door, and climbed up to where Dutchess was now laying on the ground. She was gasping for air, with her neck held fast to the tree. I had to be careful, for a dog fighting for its life, doesn't really recognize friend or foe and will bite either.

"Dutchess," I shouted, "stop...settle down, girl!" I grabbed her around the belly to avoid her teeth and lifted her up with my left arm. That freed up my right arm to quickly unwind the chain leash. It worked, but poor Dutchess sneezed and coughed intermittently for an hour, trying to rid herself of the resulting discomfort in her neck and snout. It was a very close call for my furry friend.

Life Lessons

"Safe and secure," that's what I recall a recent advertiser on television saying about its home security system. Other ads I've seen in the past included, "fool proof," burglarproof," "rest easy," "best protection," etc., but all of these systems can be breeched by a smart criminal. Toys are another example, where companies try to keep a child from using their product in an unusual way, which brings harm to them. So, is there really anything that won't break down, fall apart, cause pain or allow someone to get hurt?

The "run" we had devised for Dutchess was as safe as we could envision it to be, but we just overlooked a simple possibility. Life is simply *insecure* in so many ways. Sure, seat belts help to avoid injuries, warnings on drug labels help, too, and a police presence tends to keep criminals away. School monitors help young kids from getting hit by cars, in-school guards keep unsavory kids from bullying others or selling drugs, and hall locks help keep kid's things from getting stolen. But, no one, ultimately, can be safe and secure, right? Someone always overlooks some little thing, and then a problem occurs.

God says we are to place our *trust* in him, not in our own ability to secure ourselves from harm. This doesn't relieve us of all responsibility, of course, because using seatbelts, reading labels, having police, employing monitors or guards and installing locks *does help*....most of the time. All these are wise things we can responsibly do to ensure safety and security.

So, placing our trust in the Lord isn't something we use *in spite of common sense*. Still, it's assuring to know that *"In all things God works for the good of those who love him..."* (Romans 8:28 NIV). "In all things" means he's always working behind the scenes. If we know this and ultimately rely upon that truth, *along with* making wise choices, he promises to allow good to happen.

So, be discerning and responsible, but never "lean" (trust, rest in or rely upon) your our own understanding in anything. Instead, place your *full and complete trust* in the heavenly Father's love for you in Christ (see Prov. 3:5,6). *Now...that's a dog-gone good security system!*

"Difficult Times"

"Mom….what's wrong?"

"Ned…I just don't feel so well. I called the doctor, and he'll be over soon."

After the doctor had come and gone, mom explained to us what was happening. She had contracted what was called "Walking Pneumonia." That meant that the Pneumonia wasn't as bad as it could be, but still bad enough to make her stay in bed and take penicillin for a period of weeks in order to get better. She must  have overworked herself physically in the business of building a new home and became susceptible to the virus.

I remember, however, the day that the doctor stopped over to give her the *first* penicillin shot. He gave her the shot and then chatted awhile, as he often did. After a few minutes, he got up, took his bag and proceeded to leave, with me walking alongside.

"Ned….Ned…help me! Doctor, please come!" came my Mom's shrill voice from inside. Both of us looked at each other, turned quickly and ran back to see what was the matter.

"She's having a Penicillin reaction," he mumbled and began searching for something in his black bag. "Here it is," he said, relieved.

I don't know what shot he gave her, but it brought her relief from the sudden and painful reaction she was having to that shot of penicillin. Not many have such a reaction, but mom did, that's for sure. From there on, she was given a substitute antibiotic, which wasn't as strong, but it did help rid her of the congestion in her lungs in the weeks ahead.

As mom recovered, I still remember how weak and tired she looked, as she lay in bed. Her breathing was laborious, and she couldn't talk for very long. As a young boy, I really didn't understand how bad things could have gotten....she actually could have lost her life either in the penicillin reaction or just in trying to kick her bout with Pneumonia. Dad often sat by her, offering encouraging words and support. I'm sure he must have asked himself things like, *"Have we come all this way together, just to be separated in the end? Why would God take away the one person I love so dearly, while we were building our dream house?*

So, the fun times of my cabin life was pausing for a season of difficulty and reflection. An unplanned and uncomfortable "bad health storm" had fallen upon us quickly in our new home in the Connecticut woods, and we prayed that mom would survive it.

Thankfully, mom did make it through that stormy weather. In the weeks ahead she regained the strength she had lost so quickly, and before long all of us were back to our cabin life with its house-building plans and projects.

Life Lessons

As a child, I never fully realized how close mom had actually come to going to her eternal home. I'm glad the Lord gave her a long and mostly happy life from then on.

A question for all of us to ponder for a few moments is this: Are *you* ready to be thrust into the presence of Almighty God? Mom knew Christ as her Savior and was ready, if the Lord called her to heaven. But...*how about you?*

There are so many strange things that happen, when we least expect them, like broken ankles or automobile accidents, etc. Such things can shock us severely, like hearing that a close friend suddenly died, or you've just lost your job, or the Doctor informs you that the x-ray was positive for cancer. These are "shockers" that we just aren't prepared for and can send us into a spiritual spiral.

I remember getting a phone call in the middle of the night. I was groggy and couldn't speak clearly, but I mumbled, "Hello?"

"Ed, this is Dave. And, I've got some bad news."

At that moment my stomach leaped into my throat with fearful anticipation. If you're a mom or dad, your brain scrambles to remember where your kids are and are they safe. My kids were safe in bed, but the caller continued.

"It's Steve; he passed away at 1:00 AM." That news greatly saddened me, for Steve was one of my best friends at the time. At the funeral later that week, we celebrated Steve's life, for he had come to Christ about five years before. He was active in church and always shared his faith with others.

I could go on about an Elder in our church that lost his teenage son, or another friend of mine, whose daughter lost a two year old child to a strange birth defect. Age, intelligence, popularity.... nothing can stop the knock of death upon anyone's door, when God's timing determines it will happen.

How about you? If you're *not* a believer, then I suggest that you ask Christ into your life as Savior and Lord. He wants to forgive your personal debt of sin, save your soul for all eternity, and restore you to spiritual health. On the other hand, if you *are* a believer, but significant disobedience has crept into your life, then confess those things to him and start out again, clean and committed. Either way, the Bible says, *"If we confess our sins, he is faithful and just and will forgive us our sins..."* (I John 1:9 NIV)

For all of us...God's medicine cabinet is the Bible, and it's full of powerful and healing principles. The good news is that it never causes bad reactions or painful results, if you understand and apply his prescriptions responsibly. *Are you taking your medicine?*

Number Eleven

"I think she's pregnant," said mom, as she looked at Dutchess. We were enjoying the fading warmth of the setting sun, while Dutchess was stretched out on the lawn sleeping.

"No kidding," I replied and went over to inspect her more closely, gently rubbing her growing, furry white tummy.

"Gee…I think you're right. Where will she have them?"

"Well, I'm not sure." Mom and Dad discussed the matter for a while, and it was decided that we would create a small pen in the far corner of the unfinished dining room for her to have her pups. At this point, both wings of our new home were up, but the insides were still rough and incomplete. The dining room itself was still being wall-boarded, with the rough, wood flooring still remaining.

Another thing we discussed: "Who was the father?" There was a large, Chow dog that would often wander by the cabin, when we first got there and still did occasionally, when Dutchess came into season. So, we figured that was probably the dog that had done the deed. This meant that the pups would not be pure bred, of course, and that meant that we would not be making a lot of money later on, when selling them. We would most certainly have to sell them, for we didn't want a bunch of puppies growing up quickly and us having to feed them all (I mentioned keeping the pups, suggesting it would be a lot of fun…but they stifled that idea rather quickly).

So, about 63 days later in the fall of the year, Dutchess had her first litter of pups. At the time, it was an eye-opening experience for a little guy like me. That day began with Dutchess nervously wandering around the outside of the house, plump and ready to deliver; but we didn't exactly know *when*. I had prepared a little blanketed area in one corner of the dining room for her to have the puppies, but she didn't understand that, I guess. She seemed determined to continue wandering and scratching around outside, which indicated that it was about time for the big event. So, we brought her in and kept her in the prepared pen overnight.

Next, morning...a Saturday...the time had come. Dutchess was acting very strange, getting up and lying down, and pacing all around her pen. Finally, she lay down and began delivering her puppies....one, two, three....all the way to eleven. She was careful to lick and caress each one as it came out and to clean up the afterbirth.

Each little pup would fit comfortably in the palm of one hand, with tiny, wrinkled faces and tightly closed eyes. Each one squirmed along, struggling to move in the direction of mommy and, most importantly...food! As usual, the last pup was the smallest and, most probably, the weakest. I noticed that Dutchess kept nudging and licking the little guy, trying to jumpstart his quest for a nearby nipple. But, strangely, it didn't move.

After giving it time, I moved over and gently picked up the limp little body from Dutchess's nervous licking. I'd heard that one can rub a puppy's little chest gently to initiate its first heartbeat. This time, however, it didn't work. Dutchess was very busy attending to her new brood, so we quietly disposed of motionless number eleven, who never saw the light of life.

Life Lesson

Evil exists, and it brings death and sorrow...this is the message of life and of the Bible, too. In a perfect world, "Number Eleven" would have been as strong as his brothers and sisters, but that's not the world in which we live, and it's certainly not God's fault. But, occasionally, we run into people that will question why certain disastrous things happen. They blame God, even foolishly denying his existence, simply because they cannot explain why evil exists. But, most often, our problem with evil isn't that we can't explain it, but that some folks just *won't accept it.*

I remember class discussions on this in high school, college and with co-workers and here's how to wade through it all. If we believe that murders, rape, accidents, terrorism and disease are *bad* things, isn't the opposite also true, that *good* things also exist? Of course! If such was not the case, how can you call some things bad in the first place? So, one must believe in good in order to identify bad, right? And, if it is true that good and evil do exist, then there must also exist One who ultimately defines such things for us....Almighty God. Without God, there would be no true or reliable standard for even knowing right from wrong.

My point here is that acknowledging evil shows more clearly that God and his standards *do exist,* rather than the opposite. When Jesus came into the world, he told us about God, about how to have relationship with Him, and what is morally right or wrong. He also informed us that sin not only causes people to choose bad over good, but that it also brought disastrous *consequences* into the world. It brought things like aging, death, incurable diseases and physical tragedy. Jesus dealt with sin's penalty on the cross and offers us *God's solution,* faith in his Son's sacrificial death upon a cross in order to be forgiven and receive eternal life. Jesus said:

> *"I am the way, and the truth and the life. No man no one comes to the Father but through Me."* (John 14:6 NIV)

Number Eleven is just one small result of this cycle of death and destruction...sad, but true. But, for us as believers, ours is a wonderful future with Jesus in the new world yet to come.

> *"Do not let your heart be troubled, believe in God, believe also in Me. In My Father's house are many dwelling*

places; if it were not so, I would have told you, for I go to prepare a place for you. If I go and prepare a place for you, I will come again and receive you to Myself, that where I am, there you may be also." (John 14:1-2)

Someday, everyone's "number" will be called by God in the grand scheme of things, just like Number Eleven. But, genuine believers will open up their eyes on that day to see Jesus smiling and welcoming them into heaven. How about you? Will you see the light of day in *eternal* life?

The Hurricane

"Man...it's really going to hit us, this time. I didn't think it would," Dad said with surprise, as he listened to the weather report.

I was just walking by and heard his comment. "What?"

"There's a hurricane coming up the coast, but it wasn't supposed to reach this far." He now had my attention, and I became glued to the TV screen as well.

A fast-moving, powerful "nor'easter" was making its way up the Atlantic coast. Instead of going out to sea, as formerly predicted, its eye had turned due north and would reach Connecticut tomorrow.

I looked outside to see if there was even a hint of wind blowing through the trees. "Ned...you're not going to see anything now. It's supposed to come on land by mid-day tomorrow. That's when we'll see the rain and strong winds."

Now, I thought to myself that this will be something great to experience. I had only been through a small hurricane once before as a young boy. But, I did remember at that time stepping out on to the porch to feel the blowing winds and pounding rain of that small hurricane. This one, however, was predicted to be huge.

The house was still not completed at this point, but some of the windows on the side where the dining room was built needed to

60

be protected from flying debris. In addition, there were several tall windows stretching from floor to ceiling in the old cabin part of the house, which was now a large living room.

"We better get some wood to cover the front windows," Dad said with determination. "Let's see what we've got hanging around in back. Otherwise, we've got to go to Heinz's Hardware and get some 4X8' sheets of plywood."

Fortunately, there were several large pieces of plywood at the back of the house left over from remodeling the cabin. We brought them to the front and nailed them over the front windows. Dad didn't have enough wood to cover every window, but what we had would help.

The rest of the day went fast as we "hunkered down" for the main event coming tomorrow. Would all our preparations hold strong against the immense power of nature? We slept uneasily that night, but we were hoping for the best.

I awoke early the next morning, jumped out of bed and looked out my window. School was closed for the day in expectation of the storm, but there was only darkness and light rain at this point.

After a quick breakfast, I flipped on the TV. I kept going back and forth from station to station to catch what was happening and what was supposed to happen. Before long the winds were really picking up and the rain was coming down faster and harder. The trees in front were moving around quite a bit, with leaves and small twigs scattering about. But, it would still be a couple of hours before things got bad. And, bad it got!

Finally, the storm hit land and the force of it brought a wall of frothing, churning water onto the coastal roads and beaches. Pictures of the surging waters hitting stone walls and spraying high into the air were amazing to watch on the TV.

Soon, things really kicked up. I decided to step out into the wind in sort of a protected area by the back of the house so I could get a better feel for myself. Large trees all around were bending significantly. The tops of the brush and small seedlings were bending almost parallel to the ground as the torrential winds blew them sideways. Debris was now all around as leaves, branches and occasional heavy limbs had broken off and fallen. The wind couldn't push me over where I was, but it was still very strong and ominous.

Then, a strange thing happened over the span of just a few minutes. Everything settled down, leaving only a gentle breeze blowing through the trees. I walked to the front of the house to inspect the damage and found myself enjoying the peaceful, quiet stillness in the air. The sun was even shining through an immense portal of blue sky surrounded by dark gray clouds.

"You've got about 20 minutes, Ned," warned Dad, who was now standing nearby and looking at things for himself. He was referring to the eye of the storm, which we were now experiencing. It would soon pass over us, allowing the backend of the storm to renew its fury once again. And, soon it did just that.

Looking back at it, after the entire storm had passed, I'm not sure which end of it had been worse. Nevertheless, our renovated, cabin home had indeed survived. There were some torn shingles and a lot of tree-type debris scattered around, but no broken windows or uplifted roofs. God had protected us from harm, for which we were thankful.

Life Lessons

Life can be so much fun, and an adventurous guy like myself enjoys taking risks in order to experience it to the full. The power of a hurricane is just awesome to see and feel. I've never been in an earthquake, a landslide, a flood or a tornado, but there's an immature part of me, I guess, that would still like to experience it. And, I suppose that many have a similar desire deep inside of them. That's probably why I like Disney World so much...you can step into these crazy rides and imagine what such things would really be like. Unfortunately, such "Disney stuff" is just for fun, because real life catastrophes are not pleasurable, and can bring real destruction and death.

I've always found, however, that my life with Jesus is, at times, a spiritual adventure. I get excited about seeking God's will for my life each day, wondering how God will direct me and use me for his glory. Do you remember what Jesus said?

> *"I have come that they may have life and have it to the full."* (John 10:10 NIV)

As believers, you and I can look forward with expectancy to whatever happens, because what happens is ultimately in our Savior's hands. And, he says that he is working in every event - in everything that's pleasant and in everything that might be painful - in *everything* for good (Romans 8:28). Now, if God *is* good, which he is, and he's *working for* good in our lives, I ask you, "What's better than that, right?"

If you want adventure, think about God's awesome power, knowing that it's directed lovingly toward every believer. Stop worrying over what kind of stormy weather will soon be blowing into your life. *God is in control...*so resign as the Master Designer of the Universe. Do your part, as I've said before, but remember... he's got you covered, regardless of the stormy weather moving into your life.

Design Flaws

"That's not going to work," announced Uncle Rene, and Dad came over to inspect the cabin walls along with him.

It was now spring and the wings of the house had been added to each side of the cabin. There was still much to do inside…painting and wallpapering, as well as finishing up the counter tops in the kitchen. The polished, hard wood flooring still hadn't been installed yet either, so the months ahead would be busy ones.

"Is it useable at all?" Dad asked

"Not a chance. The old wood is just too rotten and weak."

1.   So, that was that. We'd have to tear down that old cabin to the ground, put in a secure foundation, and then add new walls and a roof. It's an understatement to say that Dad wasn't happy, for he didn't have a lot of disposable money. He'd have to go to the bank and increase the mortgage to al

low for this new build. It also meant uncle Rene would have to come down a couple of weeks more, and that meant more time and money being used up, too. Oh well, you've heard of Murphy's law?

Watching that old cabin being taken apart over the next week wasn't easy. Our family really enjoyed cabin living in all its simplicity, with its bug inhabitants, pine bark exterior, bunk beds, stone fireplace, outside pump and strange sounds in the night. But, just as quickly, the new living room was built in its place.

Unfortunately, there was another mistake we encountered, when we had previously attempted to build the bedroom wing of the house. Underneath it, my parents wanted a *full* basement, but they failed to check out the depth of the soil. They were shocked when the excavating machine dug down to about 6 feet and encountered a large, impenetrable  shale deposit. That reddish, layered stone was quite brittle and nearly impossible to chop through. After a rainstorm, puddles of that rusty-colored water tarnished everything it washed over. We dug down a few more inches, but then had to give up going any deeper. So, the basement would exist, but it would just be shorter than desired.

But, there was still another issue. Underneath the rest of the house, there was also no basement, only a small, 2 foot high crawl space. But, without having a poured cement flooring on the ground, moisture would build up over time and seep into the wood foundation. This mistake was a whopper.

Here's the problem. What do you do when you need to replace the water pipes or wiring in that small, crawl space? Such things would be very difficult to access, right? Secondly, over the years various critters dug their way under the cement blocks looking to make a home down there....wood chucks, bees, squirrels, rats, mice, rabbits, chipmunks, weasels, etc. Though I'm sure we could have had more of a problem with critter infestation than we ever did, I'm sure the "Kenerson hotel" was often visited from time to time underneath our own living quarters above.

Thirdly, not having a basement on the rest of the house created a problem years later. Though we had long moved away, and I was an adult, I visited that house several times. At one point, it was up for sale for over 3 years, and no one wanted to buy it. Apparently, the wood had rotted at the foundation level, shifting the whole house, due to *not* having full basement walls. Eventually, the sellers had to rip up all the floors and repair the entire structure in order to sell it. The outside was eventually restored, and the inside was refinished to the point of being a beautiful house worth as much as three quarters of a million dollars (2005).

Life Lessons

Mistakes happen...that's understandable. But, some mistakes can be very costly, particularly if they are spiritual in nature. I can tell you that if my parents had stayed in that house, by the time full repairs were needed, they wouldn't have had enough money to do what the real estate people did in order to sell it.

Do you make mistakes? We all do, of course, so that's really a silly question. We make practical mistakes like the above, but here are some mistakes one should try to avoid in his/her Christian life:

- Using foul, hateful, prejudicial or judgmental language.
- Getting high on drugs or intoxicated with alcoholic beverages.
- Having sexual relationships outside of a marriage commitment.
- Stealing, cheating, lying or other avenues of dishonesty.
- Enjoying or being violent toward others; bullying.
- Entertainments that glorify indulging any of the above.
- Not having a daily quiet time of Scripture reading and prayer.
- Getting lazy and not attending weekly church activities.

Keep a mental checklist of where you might have failed in these areas and prayerfully attempt to do better in the weeks ahead. Seek God's help and the help of respected friends or church leaders as needed along the way. And, always remember an important key to walking in relationship with God:

> *"Draw near to God, and He will draw near to you..."*
> (James 4:8)

The Teenage Years

The cabin was eventually transformed into a beautiful home, but this country boy still had a lot of learning experiences ahead of him. You'll see in the pages ahead how this unique, country living continued to shape my personal and family values. I hope you enjoy these fun and unique years as much I did living them.

The Baseball Champ
and The Basketball Bully

I really enjoyed sports, playing in town baseball leagues and shooting rounds of golf during the summer months with my friend, Joe. Our youth group also had a boys team that played in the town league and represented our church.

I remember one summer camp that most of our team attended. We all thought we were pretty good, of course, and liked to stroke our egos by recalling all the great plays and scores we made in the past. This particular camp was nestled in the foothills of the Adirondack mountains, and its Director was a fellow named Dr. Phil Hook. He challenged us to a game in front of everyone who attended the camp and, since we thought we were so good, we took the bait. What we *didn't* know was that he was a former soft ball pitching *professional* and formally one of the best "windmill" pitchers on the East Coast!

At the playing field, we were fired up and wanted to squash this "old" guy, who dared to challenge our reputation. But, he surprised us, saying he only needed four other players on his team.

We looked a bit befuddled. "What do you mean?" we asked.

"I only need a catcher, one outfielder, a shortstop, and a first baseman. And, I'll try my luck at pitching," Phil replied.

We chuckled inwardly, *assuming* the game would be over in no time…and it was. But, not the way we figured.

When Phil strode to the mound and warmed up, all of us just about barfed up our breakfast! If you blinked when he released the ball, it would just flash into the catcher's mitt.

WHAM…WHAM…WHAM…3 swings, fella, *you're out!* The spin he put on the ball made it curve a foot in any direction…then over the plate. All of us faced him for the first four innings out of a five inning game with knees shaking so much they sounded like a drum corps practice! Man…was he incredible!

Now, on my last up to the plate, I really didn't want to continue being so obviously embarrassed in the presence of my friends. But, I also knew I had *no chance* of hitting that ball with any predictability. But, I noticed that Phil rarely missed the strike zone. So, I decided to just casually swing the bat in the center of the strike zone, hoping the ball would hit my bat instead of me trying to hit the ball.

"Alright, see if you can put it down the plate this time," taunted this rather nervous, but mouthy teenager!

I set up, looked at the mound and Phil released his usual bullet. I just firmly slid the bat into the strike zone and…*"boom!"* The speed of the ball hitting the bat sent the ball flying over his one fielder's head far enough for me to make it around the bases. I couldn't believe it…a homerun! Of course, it was sheer luck *(funny, though, I don't remember mentioning that to anyone!)*

There was another sport, however, that I wasn't very good at …basketball. Nevertheless, I thought I could practice enough to make the cut. It was a Saturday morning and the tryouts were at the High School for a place on the team. Cheshire High had a great team, so I wanted to give it my best.

One guy, John, was a well-known player and a real tough kid. He was strong, nasty and aggressive. He was well-known as a bully, so you didn't want to cross him.

Well, I was playing him close and cutting him off from running to the basket for his easy layups. He didn't like that very much, I guess, and faked a pass to someone on my right. When I looked back at him I met the ball square in my face! He obviously threw it directly at my nose, from which I bled profusely. Though no one would accuse him of it, he was well known for that type of thing. Because of his size, he was quite able to bully anyone he wanted to. Anyway, I decided to stick to baseball after that!

Life Lesson

We've all been there, right? You know, someone stronger bullies us, someone smarter puts us down, or someone socially higher up rejects us…and it hurts. But, the answer is not to fight back with weapons from our own physical or verbal arsenal. Most often, even if we did, it wouldn't change the outcome anyway (I couldn't fight my way out of a paper bag!).

At my High School, all school-related disputes were to be settled at "the tree." That was a large oak in a corner of the school property, where guys would fight it out after school. Now, self-defense is one thing, but planned fighting is another. And, Jesus tells us that Christians aren't to be settling disputes by fighting.

> *"My kingdom is not of this world. If it were, my servants would fight to prevent my arrest…"* (Jn. 18:36 NIV)

As believers in Jesus Christ, we are citizens of God's kingdom on this earth, and our lives are to be marked by loving attitudes and kind deeds. So, apart from defending ourselves individually or as a nation, "the tree" way of resolving disputes was definitely not an option. But, the Apostle Paul also reminds us:

> *"The weapons we fight with are not the weapons of the world. On the contrary, they have divine power to demolish strongholds."* (II Cor. 10:4 NIV)

This is a more practical guideline for each of us. Paul is saying that while the citizens of this world use name-calling and general violence to get their way, these should not be *our* weapons of choice (though we might feel like it, right?). No, our weapons are more powerful, frankly. We think better, therefore, we act better. We choose to focus upon *God's will* and control ourselves appropriately. That's not always an easy thing to do, of course, especially when given a bloody nose by a basketball bully. I could have verbally escalated it or started something further that I couldn't finish, but I only would have gotten myself in deeper trouble.

So, when bullied, threatened or put down, understand that such a person is only acting out their own immaturity…young person or adult. Instead, *seize your mind* and its desire to retaliate with verbal or physical force. Tell yourself, *"I have nothing to prove here."* In so doing, you will become a genuine model of what it means to be a Christian.

I've found that it takes more courage and personal strength to *resist an urge* to hurt someone who has just hurt you, than it does to "fight back." Even if you think you can "pound him into the ground," resist doing so, okay. Why? Because, it's not about us, it's about serving Christ first.

As the Disney song says from their award winning movie, Frozen, *"Let it go!"*

Shoe Box Lane

"I'm scared," moaned Doug nervously.

"Don't be a drip," "Nothing bad ever happens in the day," responded Steve. Still, I still noticed that Steve was taking an extra-cautious  look around him as we walked through the woods.

My friends and I were hiking through a forested area about 5 miles from the house. The terrain was hilly and deeply wooded, and we were following a very narrow and winding dirt road called, "Shoe Box Lane," which broke off from the main road. It was quite overgrown with shrubs and grass, and near a large reservoir, where I sometimes went fishing with my dad. Very few people would attempt to drive their cars on it any longer, mostly because they would probably get stuck in the mud or slide off into the bushes.

On this day, the woods were quite dark, and the sun only occasionally peaked through the clouds. It was summer and hot, with a strong breeze jostling the trees. We had just hiked about a hundred yards into the thick woods up Shoe Box Lane.

Knowing the eerie and bad reputation of the area only made us more daring in our desire to explore it. Supposedly, as legend would have it, a teenage couple had decided to pull off the main road at night and had driven a short way into a place, where they could be alone. After a while, they failed to notice a dark creeping figure moving toward the back of their old Chevy. Suddenly, the strange intruder banged on the window, scaring them mercilessly. They screamed, while the boy madly tried to start the car, but to no avail.

Crack! The man drove an axe through the windshield with one, determined swing. It's said that the two frightened teens jumped out of the passenger side of the car and started running for their lives....but, they just couldn't run fast enough to avoid the cutting edge of that well-sharpened axe. Without highlighting any further details, the two teenagers...supposedly...were overpowered and met their end swiftly. Later on, the incident became known as the "shoe-box murders," because of where some of the gruesome remains were stuffed. To this day, Shoe Box Lane scares the willies out of the local residents, and few would dare take on its reputation...of course, unless you were three wide-eyed, scared but daring young twerps trying to impress some girls.

"I'm not sure about this," cautioned Kathy, as we walked along. She actually lived in a development not too far away, but had never wandered this close to the place of the crime.

"Let's go back, guys," urged Kathy's friend, Cindy. "After all...what if the story *is* true?"

"Please, it's just a lot of nonsense, that's all," I responded, being sure not to show my own uneasiness. At that precise moment a loud and odd rustling sound continued from the other side of a nearby gully. Everyone turned, listened, and watched.

"What was that?" whispered Cindy, who momentarily stumbled into the bushes along the pathway. We all wondered whether it was just a deer or a dog walking nearby. Or, was it someone creeping up behind us and...

"Let's go, guys...I'm outa here," declared Kathy. She turned and started jogging back toward the main road. All of us quickly followed, while keeping a worrisome eye on that gully. We made it to the main road much quicker than when we came, that was for sure.

Piling into the car parked at the edge of Shoebox Lane's blocked entrance, we laughed at our short, but exciting adventure. We had something to pass along to all our friends...a time when we challenged evil with courage and skill (which, of course, differed greatly from reality!)

The story of Shoe Box Lane is hard to verify, quite frankly. But, the fear we experienced in our confrontation with it *wasn't.* The story might be true, or it could just be a legend built up by two frightened teenagers going somewhere and doing something they shouldn't have. Regardless, *I really didn't want any part of it again!*

Life Lessons

Why is it that we tend to do or watch things that scare us....like watching a movie about crazed, blood-thirsty zombies over-taking our neighborhood? Halloween, for instance, is mostly just fun today, but it was built upon a sect of Celtic people called the Druids, who really believed that some of these rituals would rid them of demonic influences. Though not true, of course, it shows that mankind tends to make up things to deal with what it doesn't know.

Carved pumpkins and jack-o-lanterns can't chase demons away, nor does a silver bullet kill a werewolf, which doesn't exist in the first place. But, see a good movie about such things and you may be spotting one behind every bush in the woods!

Human *religions* are like that, for they take what they think, but don't really know about God, and then make up all kinds of things to do to please Him. For instance, Mohammed, for all his talk about peace, was more of a potentate than prophet, who killed thousands in his day to promulgate his religion by force upon others. Confucius was just a politically motivated teacher, whose fairly wise teachings, were forced upon others through his own

74

position of power in government. Buddha was probably the most humble of the three, but died while saying he was still searching for what is true. *Religions* often have their roots in some sort of violent, political overthrow of one people by another, with some degree of religious teaching associated with it.

Here's some good news...Christianity *isn't a religion, it's a relationship* with God through faith in Christ as Savior and Lord. Buddha, Confucius, Mohammed and others have struggled to understand life, yet eventually died, as all men do. But, Jesus, fulfilled over 300 prophesies that predicted his coming hundreds of years before his time. He also claimed to be the Son of God, performed historically recorded miracles and then rose from the dead....all so you and I could trust in him for eternal life. Jesus is as real as you and I, my friend, and opens up his arms to all of us:

> *"If anyone chooses to do God's will, he will find out whether my teaching comes from God or whether I speak on my own."* (Jn. 7:17 NIV)

If you're a believer as I am, we certainly don't follow *men's* ideas about God, for we follow *God's instruction to us.* Jesus came into the world to inform us of why we're here and what God, the Father, wants from us in order to receive salvation and eternal life (Hebrews 1:1-3).

At Halloween, pumpkins barely light up a dark room, but Christ is the light of the world. *Think about that!*

Musical Fun

"You know, Ed, you can play with our town band, if you want to. We could use some musical 'young blood.'"

I looked up at my friend's father. "Wow, do you think I'm good enough?"

He gave me an encouraging look. "Listen, you're better as a teenager right now than I ever will be." He was  probably right, though I didn't know it at the time. Dennis, his son and my friend, suggested I give it a try, too. Both of them were members of the Cheshire Town Band, so I said yes and showed up the following week. It was really great.

Dennis played the tenor saxophone and his father played lead trumpet. This small group of about 20 players, mostly adults, practiced every Wednesday night on the second floor of the old, red-brick, Town Hall building.

Now, downtown Cheshire was nothing more than a hilly little intersection with a few buildings surrounding it...a pharmacy, a tailor, a pizza place...as I mentioned before. Directly across the street from the corner pharmacy was a well-known boys school, called Cheshire Academy, graduating some prominent political figures, who you'd recognize today. A few hundred yards down the road in the other direction was the Cheshire Theater, which held a whopping crowd of about 50 when full! There was a well-manicured green at the center of town, which was surrounded by a couple of old, New England style homes.

Anytime someone strolled by the town hall on a Wednesday night, he or she could hear John Phillip Sousa's and other big band composers' music pouring out the open windows on that second floor. Yes, Cheshire life was easy going, conservative and mostly quiet...other than Wednesday nights, of course!

I was also in the Cheshire High School band and Jazz Band. On a sunny memorial day in May, my band director asked me to play "Taps" at the opening of the Memorial Day festivities at the high school lawn. People gathered on both sides of main street waving colorful flags, until the announcer shouted, "Now, let's all be quiet for the traditional playing of taps by Mr. Ed Kenerson from the high school band." At that point, the crowd of over 700+ stopped talking in quiet reverence, while I played that soulful song. My knees shook and my body tensed up in nervous expectancy, but I performed it without recognizable error.

By the way, did you know that "Taps" was incorporated as a standard call at military funerals after 1874 and is still used at most solemn events today, such as funerals? Most people don't know that the words to the first stanza are as follows:

Day is done, gone the sun
From the lakes, from the hills, from the sky
All is well, safely rest, God is nigh.

In my early years, Memorial Day seemed to me to be just people reminding themselves of older days. Now, since 9/11, the middle eastern wars, and all the radicalized Islamic terrorism taking place, all of us have grown to recognize the genuine honor involved in serving one's country in military service. We can thank God for those who have kept our nation safe from foreign invaders. As the song says, they serve as God's hand of safety.

Again, from elementary school through high school I played in the various school bands and local symphonies. I remember my private lessons teacher having me try out for a soloist position with the New Haven Symphony. I was the only brass entry, but there were pianists from all around the state competing for the title. On that contest day, when I stood alone on stage, I looked out to an empty concert hall except for three judges sitting stoically in the middle of the auditorium. They gave the sign to begin, and I started playing my solo. The performance went well, but I was so nervous, I bet I could have won *"the person most likely to collapse"* award.

A week later my teacher informed me that I had genuinely won over all the pianists' performances. Unfortunately, he went on to explain, because the contest was actually open *only for pianists*, it was an honor that could not be awarded to me.

I was shocked! It turned out that my teacher had known about this beforehand. Nevertheless, he wanted me in the competition just to learn how to compete and grow as a musician. I've always thought that to be an unacceptable answer. However, though disappointed, I didn't hold it against him (at least for very long!).

Life Lessons

Have you ever been disappointed like I was? You have high expectations about something, and then things fall apart. Maybe you expected a better grade on an exam, or a well-deserved job promotion. Perhaps your batting average should have been higher on the baseball team or town softball league. Whatever the case, what you wanted didn't happen. So, what do you do?

It's not fun to be disappointed, that's for sure. But, Christian or not, all of us have to grow up and deal with frustrated expectations…it's a regular slice of life. But, for the Christian, there's more to it than that, for we look to God for his leading in our lives. So, whether things go well or not, there's something in the back of our mind that says, "Okay, it must mean that *God* did (or didn't) want that to happen." And, that's a healthy attitude to have.

But, I would add something…*learn from it, too.* God isn't just mechanically pulling strings in heaven for this or that to happen.

Much of what happens comes by way of our own choices as well. Discovering why something happens to us is key to acquiring the necessary life skills and knowledge for success at school, work, church, marriage or in our personal walk with Christ. We are asked to plan and work energetically in all things, without being lazy, while we ultimately seek God's will in everything we do.

"To man belong the pans of the heart, but from the Lord comes the reply of the tongue." (Pro. 16:1 NIV)

Keep in mind, however, some things *do occur* in which we may have had no real involvement at all...a sudden sickness or loss, for instance. That's when it's particularly important to trust in God's providential care over you, for he knows what he's doing. Be confident, knowing that even Satan had to ask God's permission to bring some difficult trials into Job's life. Learn to thank God in all things, for the good and the "bad." (Col. 3:17)

Finally, also remember that *God has expectations of us.* So, keep focused on what he asks of you and work diligently at it. You certainly don't want to be suddenly disappointed at Christ's coming, because of laziness, worldliness or indifference, right?

"You also must be ready, because the Son of man will come at an hour when you do not expect him." (Luke 12:40 NIV)

The Train To Washington

"Where's your axe?" a fellow band member asked, as he hoisted his suitcase onto the bunk on the train. Axe was a common term for whatever your musical instrument was.

"I already put it up on my bunk across the aisle.... over there." I pointed to a small, fold-down bunk bed with black curtains already drawn closed.

"Good," he said grinning at me. "Your mom said for us to watch over you, so don't wander away for too long, kid." All of the other 75 band members on this train were with the Governor's Foot Guard Band of Connecticut, and except for me, all were adult men. It was 9 O'clock at night, January 19th, 1965, and we were on our way to participate in the Presidential Inaugural Parade in Washington, DC, for President Lyndon Baines Johnson. My trumpet teacher had just got me in as the soloist with the band for a year. I enjoyed performing with the band in the summer park concerts in various towns, but this trip was really going to be out of sight for me.

The Governor's Foot Guard Band had a history dating back over 200 years, with a variety of activities, including escorting dignitaries, presenting the Colors at various activities, marching in parades, and entertaining veterans, etc. Though it had at one time been involved in actual military activity, it now had just an entertainment role around the state. I was humbled at my young age to be able to play in the band with such a history.

Each sleeping berth was quite small…smaller than the wooden bunk in that old cabin. And, each car probably had about fifteen berths in it, with a passage way up the middle. I was in an upper berth, so I could look outside the tiny window while traveling.

I hung around for quite a while, listening to the guys tell their stories about past concerts and *bad soloists* (they said it grinning and looking my way!) and other crazy things that happened while performing. Soon we decided to turn in, which I was happy to do. I climbed into my berth and pulled the covers up, while glancing out the window. Everything was flying by, and the click-clack-click of the train speeding on its tracks quickly droned me to sleep.

"Up and at 'em, 7 AM it is!" exclaimed someone as he pulled my bed curtain slightly open. I couldn't believe I had over slept.

From here on, all of us were on a fixed schedule…get ready, eat breakfast and assemble in the train station at 8:00 sharp. From there, we boarded a bus, which took us to the green on Pennsylvania Avenue, near the White House. After exiting the bus, everyone seemed a bit confused as to where to line up, which band was first, which was second, etc. There must have been 20 bands or more….the West Point Academy Band, The Navy and Air Force Bands, and specially selected High School Bands, along with dignitaries, media people, etc. It was quite a celebration!

We finally found our place in the line-up and got into proper formation, eight across in the front with woodwinds leading, followed by the brass, then percussion. We were all dressed in these long-tailed, red, revolutionary era uniforms with tall, furry hats, which made us swelter on this unusually hot January day. Soon, the whistle blew, and we began marching in formation toward the grandstand, where President Johnson, his wife and other dignitaries were assembled behind thick, bullet proof glass.

Remember that President Kennedy had been assassinated not too long before, so there were many precautions.

The parade seemed to finish quickly, for I even don't remember pausing to look at the President, when we passed by. The band re-assembled at the finish point, chatting excitedly, and got back on the bus to begin the trip home.

By the end of the day, I was back home, returning uneventfully to "civilian" life. Here there were no cameras or news reporters, no wailing whistles or colorful flags waving in the breeze, just me, playing with the dogs on the front lawn of our home in the woods.

Life Lessons

A Presidential Inauguration hosts a lot of dignitaries, political figures and socialites, usually from around the globe. People with a large degree of notoriety or popularity are invited to sit in the grandstand with the President. Nevertheless, all of these "special" people have one thing in common...they will all eventually die and meet God, face to face. All their real or imagined popularity will no longer matter, for the most important and desirable invitation then is hearing Jesus say, *"Well done, good and faithful servant...come and share your master's happiness!"* (Mt. 25:23 NIV)

Would you consider yourself to be a popular person? Do people look up to you for something you've done or some skill that you have. That's wonderful, really, it is! But, if that's not the case with you, don't sweat it, okay. Knowing Jesus as our Savior and Lord makes us special people with God. And, if Jesus thinks we're great...and he does...that's the *only* thing that counts in the end!

Predators!

"Hey, Ed, what are you doing this afternoon?" asked my friend, John, as we were walking down the hallway after English class at the end of the day.

"Nothing special, I guess. Gotta practice, that's all. Why?"

John knew that I was referring to the trumpet. Every afternoon I spent about 2-3 hours practicing so I could be good enough to qualify for the Allstate competition, as well as play in local orchestras. Later on in life, I became good enough to travel professionally across the country. More on that later.

"Well, 3 of the guys are going over to Mr. Goodman's house. He's helping a couple of us with our science notes. Sometimes he puts a movie on, too...it's fun!" Mr. Goodman was our chemistry teacher and had been teaching at the High School for years. Everyone liked him, and he was very active in helping kids in school play productions and class sponsored events.

"Gee....I don't know, John. I guess I better not."

"Come on...it's fun, and he's a great guy," pursued John.

"Yeah, I know...but, I just can't skip practicing. I've got a band concert coming up, so....no...better not. Listen, let's run or we'll miss the bus." The conversation ended, and John never asked me again. In reality, I wasn't really interested in going over to Mr. Goodman's house anyway. I didn't like the guy very much.

A few months later, my mom was watching the local, evening news. "Ned, do you know a Mr. Goodman at your school?"

"Yeah…he's a chemistry teacher."

She went on to explain that he had been arrested for child molestation. At first, I was shocked to hear the news, but came over and listened to the remainder of the report. He had a way of gaining the friendship to some of the boys in his classes for years by helping them out on the side with their science projects. When he felt he was trusted, he would begin by showing inappropriate movies, and it would escalate from there. Before going to trial, he decided to commit suicide to avoid all the embarrassment.

So, our little town of Cheshire was now a statistic. It had been hit by the reality that evil lives everywhere. To this day, I don't know what happened to John or his friends, but I'm glad that I followed my instincts and avoided possible danger.

Life Lessons

That event taught me something about life in general. One can have good parents, a great church, plenty of good friends and a wonderful country setting in which to grow up. Nevertheless, sin doesn't take a vacation or reside only in a city. No matter where you live, sin can raise its ugly head and bring shame and sorrow. That's why the Bible says to keep a sharp eye out for those seeking to deceive us with false doctrines or ungodly behaviors, as well as the priority of maintaining a disciplined spiritual walk with Christ. Two verses come to mind in all this. The first is:

"With persuasive words she led him astray; she seduced him with her smooth talk." (Prov. 7:21 NIV)

Those that are *carnally* motivated, and that usually implies some type of immoral sexual indulgence, try to entice others to participate in their sin. Many non-believers do this, of course, but there are increasing numbers of legitimate believers, who do so, too. Why? Because they are caught up in a sin and can't remove themselves from its impassioned grasp. They eventually give up and simply look to justify it by some crazy rationalization (ie.

"...smooth talk."). Be prepared for both, because you'll probably face both.

Once these boys above got into more and more depraved types of porn or sinful behavior, they would have developed serious sexual addictions...just like Mr. Goodman had developed. On and on goes the cycle, until many are bound and suffering terrible physical, emotional and spiritual pain. So, be very careful who you listen to, for there are people, who deliberately want to use you for their own insatiable desires and intentions. My second verse is this:

"He will die for lack of discipline, led astray by his own great folly." (Prov. 5:23 NIV)

This speaks to what the Bible calls a fool. A fool gets into spiritual trouble by his or her lack of discipline. In this sense, the writer is warning us not to be simple-minded and thereby fail to *avoid* dangerous situations, evil temptations...even seductive predators of one kind or another.

I sensed something was not right about that teacher and his after school gatherings with certain boys, so I said no to John's invitation. In this way, I acted upon a mental and spiritual discipline: *"If you're not sure....don't do it."* (see Romans 14:22-23)

Predators are not behind every bush, but they can be occasionally be found in our schools, churches and elsewhere at times. And, the more powerful a position they hold, the more bold and dangerous they can be. So, if you think you're the prey, get your running shoes on quickly, okay? Remember Joseph? He ran from Potiphar's wife so fast he left his shirt in her hand! Amen.

Doing What You Want

As you can remember from the first book, I enjoyed building lots of things around the house. I built a large wall along the back of the house, a tree-fort, a cage for the dogs, a pen for the rabbits, a basketball hoop for the front yard...and many other things.

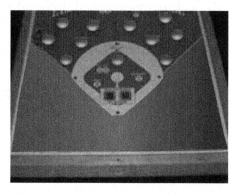

One project I remember well was building my own electronic baseball game. I saw one at the bowling alley once and thought that with my knowledge of electrical wiring I could put one together cheaply. So, I built a box type unit out of wood about the same size. The playing field was on top with holes for the ball to drop into for a single, double, triple, etc. There was even a fancy ramp to aim for in order to send a ball flying up to the homerun level. I put razor blades below each hole, which, when the metal ball dropped through, would cause the blades to touch and light up the score board. For a 12 year old kid, it was fantastic fun!

I also liked creating board games, Monopoly style, each with its own colorful graphics, attractive layouts and rules (hand drawn and colored, of course). A few of the names were "Stocks and Bonds," "Cops and Robbers," "Great Golf," "Treasure Hunter," among others. Two of them I even sent to a well-known game company, who never acknowledged having received them. It was interesting that a year or two later, I noticed two very similar games being sold in stores. They were so similar, I wondered how such a coincidence could have ever happened. Hmmm....

Today, of course, electronic/digital games for computers, tablets and smart phones are everywhere, and people rarely play board games like they used to. Still, I've got one already "on the drawing board" and ready to go, if and when the marketplace changes. Probably won't, right?

There were two other major motivations in my life....sports and playing the trumpet. I was good at baseball and always played in summer leagues, such as Little League and Babe Ruth League in the Connecticut area. Even as a little guy of 8 or so, I remember a game where I hit a simple ground ball to the third baseman easily enough to be thrown out. But, he overthrew the ball over the first baseman, so I made the turn and kept going as fast as my little legs could go. The first baseman found the ball and then threw it to the second baseman...but, he dropped it. My coach jumped up and down trying to get me to stop running, but I didn't really see him and headed for third anyway. Now, the second baseman threw it to the third baseman, who...as you are no doubt guessing...missed it entirely. So....I rounded the base for home. The ball thrown from the third baseman to the catcher was also overthrown...and I stepped on the plate for a home run! I really didn't know much about base running, other than to "keep going!" The coach enlightened me on that topic a little later.

The other strong motivation was trumpet playing. As I've mentioned before, I took private lessons, as well as played in the high school band and local symphonies. I was on track for a full scholarship in music at most any music college I would choose...but, there was a problem. I had *little interest* in music education or in becoming a music teacher, for I simply played the trumpet for my own pleasure. When I later went to college, I took a couple of introductory music classes, but found myself quite bored.

My point is this...I had to make a choice, which would not only affect my high school goals, but my college and career aspirations as well. I chose *not* to pursue music, just play the trumpet, and I'm glad that I did. Soon after, God started leading me toward ministry and later on, Seminary. This proved to be a far better choice, as it worked out. But, it was not an easy choice to make at the time, for many folks continued to urge me on in music.

Life Lessons

Doing what we like is sometimes a double edged sword. Liking something could be indicating that we have the *drive* to do it well. On the other hand, many times people try building a career around what they like, but really aren't qualified or talented enough to successfully pursue...long term. I humbly understand that I had a good measure of innate talent from God for trumpet playing. But, to have a successful music career in teaching, for instance, more was needed, not the least of which was the motivation to study it, write it and pursue a degree in it.

I remember the difficulty I had telling my music teacher about my choice to pursue other things, possibly ministry. He had me entering the Air Force Band, graduating from Curtis School of Music and becoming a great teacher. Nevertheless, he supported my decision, and poured his energy into my performing abilities.

What do YOU want in life? What motivates you and gives you a lot of personal enjoyment and satisfaction? Are you skilled enough in an area of ability to pursue it, or is your "dream" just that....a wish and a fantasy. Not all desires are spiritually sound or practically wise, contrary to popular opinion. So, when thinking about a significant step in your life like career, college, sports, etc., learn to "chew on it" for a while. Think more and "feel less" while you're doing that, for our feelings can be whimsical at times, instead of coming out of a *core motivation* (from the "real you"). Not every core motivation is from God, either, for it may be genuine, but not necessarily the best road to take.

Good choices, those that are wise, come mostly from sound judgment as opposed to emotion. They stem from what is best and praiseworthy, not necessarily from something that is just pleasurable and temporary.

In the spiritual realm, give God the right to direct your life by "praying through" a decision, leaving plenty of time to read the Scriptures and check out your decisions with people you trust. Choosing a hot dog over a hamburger at lunch won't affect your life much either way, but choosing the wrong person to date, for instance, certainly will. The same goes for typical life decisions in areas of our entertainment, sports, friendships, career choices, etc. In all this, be sensitive to God's leading, okay, for the Bible warns:

"How long, O naïve ones, will you love being simple-minded?"

Prov. 1:22)

Faking It!

It was a cold, sub-zero Friday night in January, and our church youth group had just arrived for its Winter Retreat in a well-known, New Hampshire conference center. A fresh blanket of new snow a foot thick had just fallen on  top of the already two feet covering the ground. The bus of 50 teenagers from Cheshire Connecticut had barely made it through the unsettled weather, but we were all excited and ready to have fun. Everyone located their rooms, stuffed their luggage under the bunks and headed out for skating, sledding and hot chocolate.

All of us stayed in the large rooming facility known as the "ark," which I remember as being about a couple hundred feet long and two floors high. It was like a small hotel and had enough rooms to accommodate the entire group. It was an old building with wide, pine floor boards, beat-up plaster walls, and several bunk beds to a room.

On either end of this old, wooden structure was a fire escape stairway leading from the roof down to the ground. The room I was in was an end room with about 8 bunks in it. The guys were wrestling and fooling around, when one of them suggested we go out and climb up the fire escape to the roof for fun. Well, only two of us were crazy enough to try it, so a fellow named Mike and I squeezed ourselves through an uplifted window and proceeded to the roof. The others waited below and listened as we traversed along the roof top, twenty feet off the ground.

The roof had only a slight slant to it and was covered with plenty of snow. The fallen snow did give us some traction, but not much. As we made our way along, we passed some moisture-frozen, skylight windows and decided to wipe the frost off on one of them to see what lay below.

We rubbed the glass in wide circles until the frost disappeared. Putting our noses to the glass, we peered down and had a quick, foggy view of people moving around. Mike and I had unknowingly come upon a room full of teenage girls, who looked up and saw our deformed, scary faces in the glass above them.

Suddenly, there was a massive surge of shrieking, screaming females from below! I practically fell off the roof in surprise! I don't know who was more scared, but Mike and I gathered our wits and then tore off back to the room. We slipped and fell along the way, but finally careened off the roof onto the fire escape by our window just in time to hear two adult leaders pounding on our door. They were shouting, "Hey, what's going on...who's on the roof...Kenerson...are you in there?"

Busted! Well, not yet anyway, for the room door was still locked. "Let us in...now!" the leaders demanded.

Mike and I jumped through the window and were now on the floor with 5 other guys laughing their guts out. I immediately whispered to the guys, "Hey...get around me and let's start a wrestling match...and *close that window!*" One of my accomplices attended to it quickly. Mike, in the meantime, had jumped into the shower, clothes and all. He closed the curtain and hoped no one would discover his strategy.

Well...it worked. When we let the leaders in, I think they sort of knew it must have been someone on this side of the building, but they really couldn't tell who it was. I don't recall them specifically asking if we were the culprits, but they left all of us with a warning. Mike and I escaped detection, but we remained rather subdued for the rest of the retreat…well, at least for that night, anyway!

Life Lessons

Being a teenager from the country or the city doesn't guarantee any level of common sense or maturity, as clearly seen in the above example. Though we did a lot of fun and crazy things over the years in our church youth group, *eventually* we did listen to our leaders and grew out of our prankish ways to embrace some degree of spiritual maturity.

How about you? Life can really be fun at times, can't it? Perhaps your fun is found in sports, band, academic competition, or in some other area. That's great, but, let me ask you this, *"What are you doing for Christ?"* That's what my church Youth Director shared with us all the time. It's ultimately what God is going to ask all of us, right? So, again, *"What are you doing for Christ?"* Are you growing up and getting serious about your responsibility to obey your Lord and Savior? Or, are you still focused on fooling around most of the time.

You know, fooling around with friends is one thing. You can even fool around with your schooling, your college and even your career to some degree before things finally catch up with you. But, fooling around with God and his demands over your life…that's not smart at all. I hope you're not in that tribe of believers. Here's one of my favorite Scriptural passages in this context:

"Be happy young man, while you are young,
and let your heart give you joy in the days of your youth.
Follow the ways of your heart and whatever your eyes see,
but know that for all these things God will bring you to judgment."
(Ecclesiastes 10:9 NIV)

So, it may be remotely possible to explore snow laden roof tops, escape a pack of screaming teenage girls and then effectively cover up your misguided tracks. But, sooner or later, *God will track you down*! Are you ready for that day?

Guts, But No Glory!

"Why don't you try out?" asked my friend, Joe, who was encouraging me to participate in the school wrestling tournament.

"Awe, I'm not sure I could win, that's all," I replied.

"Come on, you're one of the best in gym class. Plus, imagine the glory you'll get from wrestling in front of the entire school assembly. Hey, your popularity quotient will skyrocket, right? And, you might even be able to ask Mary Lou out on a date." Joe chuckled, knowing she was definitely "out of my class." So, I entered the contest.

It was the school's yearly wrestling tournament and all-school assembly. The two winners in each weight class in after-school intramurals got to wrestle each other in front of the whole student body. It was now the final intramural match held in a small room in the gym area between myself and this other fellow, who happened to be a senior. I weighed about 135 lbs. and he weighed about 148 lbs. So, he was heavier and also more experienced, having won the championship last year. But, I was determined and ready.

We wrestled for three periods, and he was slightly in the lead up until the last 30 seconds. He was holding me down, but I squirmed out of his grip on the floor and rose to my feet. At that critical point, we were struggling to put the other guy down, because either one could win by doing so. I crossed my right foot in front of his and flipped him onto the mat, then quickly fell on top of him. He was pinned to the ground, and I won the final, preliminary match.

All the guys watching clapped in respect for an underdog like me. The final contest between us would be a week later at the all-school assembly. I was fired up and couldn't wait!

The day before the match, I'll never forget it, across the speaker in the class room came these words, "Unfortunately, the wrestling assembly scheduled for tomorrow afternoon has to be cancelled due to circumstances beyond our control."

I sat there in English class with my mouth open in disbelief. Here was my opportunity to gain recognition for more than just my trumpet playing. It would have raised my popularity with the girls and increased my bravado quotient with the guys. Out of all the years this could have happened....why now and why me? I was just deflated.

Again, my friend Joe was quick to "encourage" me later on. "Listen, Ed, it's not the end of the world, okay. Who wants some of the prettiest and most desirable girls in the school fawning over you anyway....*how boring!*" I looked at him for a second, and he started laughing out of control, so I knew it was time to step back into reality. I was given a trophy by the coach at the end of the week, because I was the last winner in our particular match sequence. So, I did get *something* out of it after all. But, it was a trophy without applause.

Life Lessons

It's odd, sometimes, to figure out *why* we do things. I wanted to win, but I wanted to win in front of the whole school and find favor with the opposite sex. My motivations were quite mixed.

Later on, when I went to college, I played the trumpet in the college orchestra and in some churches nearby. People would complement me, as they would anyone, who had obvious skill. But, God showed me that my motives were often mixed and self-centered. When I finally learned to accept praise sincerely and wasn't so intent on always being the best, things changed. I found that I could serve the Lord better by genuinely appreciating the accomplishments of others. Competition had been replaced with a more godly attitude, which didn't demand being better than someone else.

God asks of us to love him genuinely and completely....from the heart. Mixed motives don't fly too well with him, for he wants to occupy the centermost place in our hearts. For instance, perhaps you want to be a leader in your youth group, in your college class or on a church committee. Great, but seek *God's* purposes first and foremost, not your own, and God might favor your efforts. Perhaps you want to date someone that's considered very popular. But, are you genuine in your desire to do so, or are you doing it for show or social status? How would that person really feel, if they found out you were "faking it?"

Genuine glory belongs to God, if we're seriously motivated believers. Our primary motivation should always be glorifying him in all we do. Whether or not our other motivations are acceptable, that's another question, of course. But, if we want the favor of God in the day-to-day details of our lives, we must have a sense of spiritual *prioritization.* The Bible says:

> *"...seek first his kingdom and his righteousness, and all these things will be given to you as well."* (Mt. 6:33)

And, if we're going to boast about anything, take this tip from Jeremiah 9:23,24:

> *"...let not a wise man boast of his wisdom, and let not the mighty man boast of his might, let not a rich man boast of his riches; but let him...boast of this, that he understands and knows me."*

Testing Things

I used to love running our old, rusty 1948 Chevy Coupe up and down the drive way, even at 14 years of age. Dad bought it for mom just to run to the store and back, for he didn't have a lot of money to buy another new car. It was dark  maroon and had a gas-gulping engine, though it did run well most of the time. After a snow storm, I'd try to gun it to the top of the hill, which had about a 50/50 chance of success. Otherwise, you'd have to slide backwards down the hill, while trying not to careen off into the woods. It was great fun!

However, dad junked that old beast and bought a slightly newer car, a 56 Buick, which was still old, but in better shape. It was a real boat, though safe and dependable. I would often take this car to pick up some of my friends going to youth group on Saturday nights. One winter day, I remember turning onto a side road in Cheshire, and suddenly had the thought of testing the car's ability to hold its traction on a snowy road. No one was coming in either direction, so I hit the brakes and put the car into a controllable spin at about 30 miles per/hour. I thought I'd easily correct it and stay on the road, but that old boat just couldn't hold the road....it sailed right into a ditch! When the tow truck mom called came over to pick me up, I was embarrassed to no end. The car was not damaged, fortunately, but she asked, "What were you thinking?"
"I wasn't," I responded, sheepishly.

Well, maybe a year later, our car was not available to pick up some friends for the youth meeting, but my youth director was kind enough to let me borrow his VW Beetle. I drove it to Wallingford to pick up some kids, then came back to the Baptist church in Cheshire, stopping at the light in town. I looked at the small, flat pane of glass for a windshield, and asked out loud in front of the others, "I wonder how strong this glass is in this little foreign car?" So, I tapped it with my knuckles to find out ...gently, I thought. Well, you guessed it...it cracked like a piece of thin ice! Later, I explained things to my youth director and offered to pay him back, of course, for the damage, but he declined. However, he did echo my mom's words, "Ed, no problem, but....*what were you thinking?*" I didn't have much of an answer for that one either.

Later on in college, I took a part-time Christmas job in a fine leather and jewelry store. It was a small store with glass counter cases surrounding the walls. Sales clerks, of which I was one, would simply reach into the case from behind and bring out things like watches, decorative pieces of art, and finely crafted leather goods. It was a busy time, Christmas, but this one night was slow on customers. My hands were casually resting on the 6 foot, glass top of one of the cases, when....that's right....I again inquisitively asked myself, "I wonder how strong this glass really is....and lightly pushed down on it."

Crack! The entire six foot long, clear glass top shattered into a thousand pieces all over the valuable items on the shelf below. It startled every person in the store, and they all looked up to see what had happened. I stood there trying to fade into the wall behind me, hoping my boss would think that a customer had done it, but I was the only one nearby. I couldn't believe it, moaning "*Not again!*" My boss actually had a lot more to say to me later that night, a bit more graphically expressed, perhaps, when he suggested that my services were no longer required.

Curiosity is something I've learned over the years to control. It never killed my cat, but it did cut into my expenses and reputation.

Life Lessons

Ever doubt something that you've believed in or trusted was true? I mean, I thought I could control that old Buick, but couldn't. And, the glass in my Youth Director's VW bug or in the display case at that jewelry store wasn't as strong as I figured it was. For sure, I *should* have had more common sense in those situations.

God, however, doesn't want to be tested, but believed. He's totally trustworthy and capable of meeting all of our needs, but, again, he wants us to *trust him, not test him.* We tend to say, "Show me, and I'll trust you." But, he lovingly says back to us, "Trust me, and then I'll show you."

> *"Call to Me and I will answer you, and I will tell you great and mighty things, which you do not know."* (Jer. 33:3)

Again, it's just simple faith. We want to know, test and have detailed explanations for everything. But, smart believers don't live by explanation, they live by faith. We'll never know everything anyway, so deal faithfully with what you already know is reliable and trustworthy. Otherwise, you might end up having to pay for a lot of broken glass! God says:

> *"The secret things belong to the Lord our God, but the things revealed belong to us and to our sons forever, that we may observe all the words of this law."* (Deut. 29:29)

A Life Changing Youth Group

There's a ton of churches out there, many with ideas on how to reach young people for Christ. Ours was called Cheshire Teens, and was started by a young man named Al Baines, who had a vision for sharing  Jesus Christ with teenagers in the Connecticut area. Along with his team of caring workers, they helped lead many teenagers over a twenty year period to know Christ. Time limits me from telling all the great things about these people and the program itself, but you can get the details in my book, "Reaching Teenagers For Christ: The Cheshire Teens Story." For now, let me tell you a couple of ways it impacted this country boy's life.

First, it brought into my life some great friends for life, one of whom later became my wife. I first met Kathy at one of our Saturday night outreach events, where the group did fun things like bowling, wild-goose chases, swim parties, winter weekends and summer camps. Eventually, we both became involved in youth ministry ourselves. However, during these high school years, we really were quite competitive in a fun way, and the retreats were great opportunities to out-do each other.

For example, at one Winter Retreat in upstate New York on a cold, snowy January day, the guys and I were snow-balling the girls as soon as got off the bus. Of course, they screamed, yelled and threw snow balls back at us....but, with little accuracy I might add. Later that afternoon, however, after exiting one of the meetings, we noticed that those same girls were all laughing amongst themselves in front of us guys, but intentionally so. Finally, it came out that they had gotten into our cabin and had sabotaged my luggage.

Well, we ran off to our snow covered cabin at the top of the hill to see what they had done. We stopped short just outside to see my underwear hanging on a rope - *frozen solid!* While the guys had been busy, Kathy and her crew had crept into our cabin, soaked my underwear in water and hung them out to freeze for everyone to see. They were as stiff as a board. *I had been out-maneuvered at my own game!* Later, I did have some retaliation, but my satisfaction from it never rose to the height of my initial embarrassment.

There were other, more significant Cheshire Teens' events as well…here's another. His name was Roger. He was probably in his early twenties and was only able to get around on crutches. Roger was not able to speak distinctly in conversation, because his words would mumble together. But, those patient enough to understand him, could do so. I'm not sure how he came out to the Saturday night group, but a friend must have invited him.

Roger eventually made his decision to follow Christ and was faithful in attendance at the Bible studies. He came to the Lord, I believe, because his Christian friends made the commitment to go beyond the norm. We included him in all the group activities, especially in giving him the transportation assistance he needed.

On one particular Saturday night, the Teens group went bowling, and Roger as usual came along. The whole group left after the church meeting around 8:30 PM and went over to the bowling alley to settle in, while Al cleaned up a bit at the church.

When Al did arrive at the bowling alley about a half hour later, the manager came up to him, saying, "I'm sorry, but I can't have him (Roger) bowling any longer, because the couple next to him are upset."

Al listened to his complaint. It seems that Roger could only bowl by stretching out on the floor and pushing the ball forward with his chin. The couple in the lane next to Roger and the other teens were probably annoyed or embarrassed at this, so they told the manager to move him or they would have to leave.

"I understand," Al responded. "It is somewhat awkward, I know. However, he's one of the group, and I would hate to have to take all 85 of my teenagers back to the church tonight…if Roger isn't allowed to bowl. Do you think you might be able to move that couple to another lane?" They were moved within 5 minutes. Amazing what motivates some people to do the right thing!

That was Cheshire teens….a place to have a lot of fun and a secure place to be taught about loving God and loving others through Jesus Christ. I hope you also have such a great youth group, college group or church study to attend. If you don't at present, try to find one that's spiritually solid, okay….your life will never be the same.

Life Lessons

I'm going to let one of the teenagers, who found Christ at one of our events, share in her own words, what this exciting youth program did for her. It's a life lesson worth remembering and for which I praise God every day.

"Where do I begin to explain what Teens meant and still means to me? There was that first Friday rap night about love that seemed so weird, but intriguing and drew me back to the Saturday night splash party. Then, there was the invitation from Ed to accept Christ, which I responded to. I just felt drawn to ask him what in the world he was saying in his talk about God, Jesus Christ and salvation. In the days that followed, there were those sweet hours of initial discipleship he and other friends gave to me as they came to my house and patiently explained the Word to this babe in Christ. The rest of the summer was full of Bible study, prayer, picnics, girls/guys nights, beach trips, camping, and, of

course, regular Saturday nights. I had new friends – <u>true</u> friends. (I'm reliving it all!") Such precious, heart-piercing memories put a smile on my face to this day at the recollection of it all.

Teens molded me into a new creation (II Corinth. 5:17). God used it to give me a born again family (my alcoholic Dad came to Christ two months after me!). It gave me direction and hope during a very difficult time in my troubled home life.

Teens changed my life forever. I would need to write my own book to say it all. The pure, simple, uncomplicated, uncompromising salvation message was always at the front, and never clouded with gimmicks. Leaders were always available and ready to talk, REALLY TALK to you, as well as challenge you. To everyone I say, "Thanks to all of you leaders, and to my friends who showed me love, patience and boldness to "keep a steady hum" in Christ!" (Annette)

The Slippery Slide

"You've got to be kidding," I exclaimed, as I tried to maneuver down the icy, Prospect Mountain road once again.

Some of the kids, who came out to the youth group in Cheshire, lived on the other side of a small mountain south of

Cheshire. I had a girlfriend for a while, who lived just over that ridge in the town of Prospect. In the summer, there was no problem traversing that 25 mph, severely winding road up or down for about a mile. But, in the winter you really had to worry more about the ice that could quickly freeze on it, more than the snow, for snow would always give you some traction. A light rain falling just around the freezing mark would freeze to the surface, causing unsuspecting drivers to literally slide off the road into a tree or an embankment. Uphill was certainly difficult, but downhill in the dark at 10 o'clock at night…that's another story!

"We should have gone the long way around," one of the teens said, shaking as she said it. It was, fortunately, still light out, and we were coming down that hill…very slowly.

"Gee, Ed, can't you go slower."

"I'm going as slow as I can…really….just creeping." In reality, I *was* moving very slowly, half creeping and half *sliding* on that smooth and slippery downhill road.

"Oops!" The game suddenly changed. The car was now completely sliding and turning sideways down a straight stretch of road about a couple of hundred feet long.

"We're going off the road!" someone shouted.

"Not yet....don't worry, we're okay." I mumbled, trying to encourage everyone, especially myself. Again, we weren't going fast at all. But, it was my father's car tonight, and those trees along the side of the road would really do a number on it.

"Come on!" I said angrily, trying to touch the brakes or turn the wheel in a way that would right side the car on the road...but to no avail. We had lost complete control at maybe 3 mph, and were sliding directly for the far side of the curve that lay ahead. And, that curve had a ditch on the upper side, with sheer sloping woods on the down side.

"Ed, do *something!*"

The car continued its slow but steady slide toward the trees. There was no hope in stopping the car on the road, but there was a possible way to still make the turn. Along the side of the road was a shallow, slightly snow covered ditch just before the curve and adjacent woods. I gave the car some gas and turned the wheel in such a way as to bring it around, front end first.

"What in the world are you doing?" asked one of the guys. I really didn't know for sure, but an idea just hit me. If I deliberately went off into the ditch, I'd have some traction to either slow to a stop or make the curve. That was my plan, and I didn't have time to explain.

Thud! The car's right tires fell into the ditch, dragging and bumping its underside along the way. One of the girls shrieked, and we finally slid to a stop. All of us sighed in relief. In a few moments, I released the brake, and we resumed our adventure, jumping back onto the road and continuing "safely" down-hill from there on.

Life Lessons

Slippery roads are dangerous, but have you ever just tried to cross a frozen stream or pond? You slip all over and probably end up on your seat. On the other hand, if you cross that same frozen pond after a couple of inches or more snow has fallen on it, you can cross more easily and safely. The snow tends to stick to the ice and provides a more stationary foundation upon which to cross.

In life, there are slippery places to walk and more stable places to walk. I would suggest four spiritual guidelines to help you discern what is safe and acceptable behavior, for instance.

1. Does the Bible specifically say it is wrong or right?
2. If not mentioned in the Bible, is such behavior *intentionally* pure and godly, or is its real intent to be impure and ungodly?
3. If it is basically okay, are *my motives* pure?
4. If so, will it *hurt or offend* anyone where I actually do it?

Generally, this sequence is a very constructive way of helping us discern God's moral will. Keep in mind that here will always be someone who is more liberal or conservative in their thinking. All of us, of course, need to be careful about being either too rigid or too soft in what we believe about these things. But, aim for *exactly* what the Bible teaches. Then, I would suggest that you *"lean"* to the conservative side, and you'll probably be safer. That's because we tend to allow ourselves too much freedom to indulge our human natures, and that often gets us into trouble...like trying to go down a slippery mountain road at night.

"...be diligent to present yourself approved to God as a workman...accurately handling the word of truth." *(II Timothy 2:15)*

Fisticuffs

"So...wanna try it?" Steve looked at me with anticipation.

"Okay, but let's wait until after the morning session and we're heading to the rec-hall,"

"Great!"

Steve and I, the self-appointed, infamous, high school duo for making wild & wacky things happen at our youth group, were at our summer camp at Sacondaga, New York. The group went there often for our summer retreats, and usually brought a sizeable group to run our own program with speakers, counselors, activities, etc.

Steve and I waited until the morning speaker was finished, then nodded to each other. As the group exited the chapel and dispersed, we deployed our gag.

"Look...leave me alone, you idiot!" I began, with a twist of anger.

"Sorry, *baby*...can't take it, huh?" Steve whined, escalating the pretend fight that we were brewing for fun. Some of the kids became unnerved and moved out of the way, unaware it was fake.

"Look, I said I'm not interested. Are you brainless or just deaf?" Steve was really getting into it now, and gave me a firm push. I returned the favor by shoving him a couple of feet. We now had about 30 teens around the two of us, all eager to see the two of us really go at it. The fact that we had just come out from a session where the speaker talked about getting along with each other, only added fuel to the fire. Finally, I threw a fake punch.

"Take this," Steve shouted angrily and returned with a left hook. The whole thing was choreographed, including the sound effects. As he threw the punch, he unnoticeably cuffed his other hand on his thigh for sound. I, of course, acted it out as well by dropping to the ground and grimacing. I kicked at his leg to trip him and then got up, dragging him up with me like Roy Rogers with a bad guy.

POW! I right-hooked him in the stomach and shot a punch to his face, all with the appropriate sound affects cleverly disguised. The other teens didn't know what to do, but a couple of leaders ran over to break it up. When they got there, we just burst out in laughter and exposed the gag. Of course, the leaders chased us for a quarter mile up the hill into the woods, because they were embarrassingly taken in as well. *Ah...the sweet smell of success!*

Life Lessons

It's pretty easy to "fake out" some people; we call them gullible, right? They just seem to be easily taken in by another person's charm or enthusiasm. Salespeople love to see someone like that coming into their store. "An easy mark!" they would say.

Satan is probably the best fake-out artist around, but his antics are specifically designed to hurt people, not just have some fun. And, he's also got all the sound effects, deceptive moves and cons stored away in his evil mind, just waiting to be tested on you and me. The Bible says:

> *"Satan himself masquerades as an angel of light. It is not surprising, then, if his servants masquerade as servants of righteousness. Their end will be what their actions deserve."* (II Cor. 11:14, 15 NIV)

Satan tries to fake people out by fostering fancy philosophies of life, some espoused by popular spokespeople like movie stars, political figures or college professors. At other times, he may throw difficult life circumstances at you, hoping to disable you with worry and confusion. Also, he might get you thinking about reaching out for material things or wealth in order to satisfy your desire for life happiness.

Beyond this, he's a great liar, too, and can entice us with almost magical skills at creating pleasurable images of success and sensual enjoyment. But, those who fall for such masked temptations soon end up empty and ashamed. In all of the above situations, once you start following his lead, you soon recognize his game, and it's just another empty promise. Our worth and satisfaction only come by living godly lives of contentment and Christ-likeness.

It's also important to remember that Satan can do nothing to you *unless permitted by God* (remember the book of Job?). So, for all his huffing and puffing, he is at God's mercy and under the restrictive power of God's dwelling Holy Spirit. Nevertheless, don't underestimate his ability to try to fake you out when you're least expecting it. Jesus wisely reminded his followers:

> *"Watch and pray so that you will not fall into temptation. The spirit is willing, but the flesh is weak."* (Matt. 26:41 NIV)

Dumb and Dumber

"Come on...stop "dilly-dallying" around!" shouted Charlie to the stragglers. I was with a group of 15 teenagers, who were on a return hike along route 20 from Bridgeport to Cheshire, Connecticut. We had been dropped off Friday night in Bridgeport and stayed overnight in a small, youth outreach facility. The plan  was to get up early on Saturday morning and then walk back to Cheshire, arriving at 7:30 or so for the regular Teens meeting.

The meeting the night before went off well...lots of food, billiards and fun games later on. We were somewhat nervous, however, about staying overnight in this old, renovated building where this outreach center was located. So, sleep didn't come fully until around 3 am, and we were up at 5:30 am to begin the hike.

"Hey," let's rest, Chas." That's what we sometimes called Charlie, one of our youth sponsors. Charlie was about 22 and a fantastic guy, always a lot of fun, but also a good Christian model in his spiritual life. He would lead songs at the youth meetings and spend quality time with teenagers during the week, getting to know them and sharing his faith. Many kids came to the group just because of who he was.

After about 4 hours of steady walking all of us were tired, uncomfortable and began to complain. "Come on, you guys... bunch of softies. Alright, let's take five," was his reply.

I crumbled to the ground, in desperate need of some rest. Unfortunately, I had decided to wear army boots for this auspicious event, thinking that the extra support would guarantee a timely and successful arrival. Boy...was I wrong! It only made a 20 mile trip into a 50 mile trip...according to the pain I felt in my feet, anyway. Both my calf muscles had tightened up so much I was forced to hobble along on just the upper parts of my feet. I could only take short strides or my thighs cried out, "Are you crazy!" To make it worse, I had enough blisters on each foot to pass for measles. In other words, I'd just about had it.

There were five of us who wanted to give up at this point in the walk. The others were just tired, but still wanted to continue. We had already gone about 15 miles, but we stopped at a McDonald's restaurant and indulged ourselves with some refreshments.

Finally, I moaned, looked up at Charlie and said, "That's it for me," and four others agreed heartily. Charlie looked at me and the others and sensed that the five of us were truly finished. So, he agreed. I got on the phone and called for someone to pick us up and take us home. What bothered me the most was the silly decision to wear those crazy army boots...*what a jerk I was!*

Well, the rest of the group took off, and our ride arrived shortly thereafter. We got home around 5 pm., and I jumped into the tub to soak away the pain. Two hours later, I took my water soaked body to our Saturday night outreach meeting, and, of course, was mocked out to no end by those who heard of my shortcomings. Ah...the joys of notoriety!

Life Lessons

Have you ever heard the statement: *"The best laid plans of mice and men, often go astray?"* It's from the poem, *"To a Mouse"* by Robert Burns in 1786 and means that though all of us may plan well, things can still go wrong.

Well, that's a bit negative overall, but it does have some truth to it regarding things we undertake or goals we set. It could be a

110

project at school, a new responsibility at work, or a home "fix-the-kitchen-sink" plan that literally springs a leak! The point is that planning well, though always necessary, doesn't *guarantee* that we didn't overlook some little detail that causes problems to occur.

I never figured that wearing big, hiking boots, normally geared for climbing, would cause me trouble on a long walk…but, it did. So, the first lesson I learned in this experience is to plan BETTER. There's no substitute for thinking something through first before haphazardly jumping into it. For instance, we need to plan our conversations with non-believers so that we are *"ready to make a defense to everyone who asks you to give an account for the hope that is in you…"* (I Peter 3:15). Spur of the moment answers to serious questions won't fly. Study and show yourself approved, a person who rightly handles the Word of God." (II Tim. 2:15)

We should also have a well-planned time of daily devotions with the Lord, searching his Word and deeply rooting ourselves in prayer. This is a discipline too often ignored or put off by some at great cost to their spiritual well-being. We should also consult with key people, as necessary, in order to help us in areas we are unsure about. Lastly, prepare, prepare, prepare! "Shooting from the hip" in a last minute effort to do anything will probably only bring bland performance at best and possible flat-out failure.

Overall, whether you're witnessing, ministering, studying, working or even writing a book, all should be accomplished by responsible effort, diligence and foresight. Someone has said:

> *"We are what we repeatedly do; excellence… is not an act, but a habit."*

Above all, in your plans be sure to keep seeking God's will in everything, looking patiently for his perfect leading.

> *"Commit your works to the Lord and your plans will be established."* (Pro. 16:3)

Blonde and Beautiful

"Wow," I thought to myself, as I noticed Joan scurry down the hall to class. Joan was a beautiful young girl and had the attention of most of the boys in my 11th grade class.

We'd been in the new house for quite a while now and had developed some good friends in the area. But, in the area of girl relationships, I was somewhat awkward, to say the least. Joan was one of the most popular girls in the school, well-liked, intelligent and very proper. I'd see her at occasional parties, or talked with her, if we happened to be in the same class. But, beyond that, I lacked the confidence to approach her as a friend.

For some reason, now that I was a junior in high school, I had built up enough courage to try to ask her out on a date. Why I would do this at this point remains somewhat of a mystery to me. She was certainly "out of my league" to coin a phrase. She was very social, I was not. She dated the super-cool, the popular and the sports-jocks. My only claim to fame was that I played a pretty good trumpet and played in the band at football games. Her values and lifestyle indicated that she was not a Christian girl, but I was a guy who knew Christ and whose primary interests centered around Cheshire Teens, my church youth group. She was very good looking, and I was about average, at best.

Anyway, as you've probably already guessed, she nicely turned me down. Even my pre-invitation strategy...having many open calendar dates as possibilities...didn't succeed. Strangely enough, she had *weeks of unbreakable, sequential and significant events going on in her life!* Hmmm....

I do remember two other dates that I had, that's all, through my entire high school years. One was when I asked a girl out at camp for the "Sadie Hawkins Day" banquet. She was a cute and popular Christian girl, and we had a fun time together. Another girl I went out with, I'll call her Mary, was attending the youth group for a while, but was not a believer. She had a reputation, which was not a good one, frankly, but I really didn't know that at the time. What I did know, was that she was blonde and good looking. She had been invited out by some of the girls in the youth group in hopes of winning her to Christ.

Our personalities didn't really mesh, I guess, so we never went out together again, though she did come out to the group sporadically for a while. Over the years, I learned that the leaders in the group really questioned my motivations for dating her, given her reputation and my teen leadership role in the group. Again, all I could say was, and it was true, that she was attractive, fun to be with and that we had a pleasant time together on the date.

Then, there was Kathy. She and I started going to Cheshire Teens in our freshman year in high school, though we later discovered we had unknowingly been in the first grade together. Our friendship centered in just enjoying each other's sense of humor and being comfortable around each other whereever we went. We never formally dated until college, but everyone at the youth group knew we were a "couple." If I was driving to or from Teens, she'd often be with me. If bowling, we'd be together, if miniature golfing, the same. On retreats, as I said before, we'd be in fun-hearted competition, raiding one another's cabin or trying to out-do the other person in any way we could. We laughed at the same things, talked and cared about the same things and enjoyed hanging around together where ever we were. We were two wonderful friends, who one day decided to make it a life commitment. What a blessing my Kathy has been to me!

Life Lessons

Relationships are tough, anyway, let alone those with the opposite sex. Television, movies, music...entertainment in general ...bombards us with all kinds of romantic advice for what we're supposed to do and say. So much of it, though, is most often just spiritual junk and bears little resemblance to reality. Now, this isn't a book on romance, dating or "how to select a marriage partner." But, let me suggest three key principles to keep in mind in this area of dating relationships.

First, at any age...high school, college, adult...attraction is usually where it all begins. Something draws us to another person in his/her looks and personality. And, that's good and godly.

Second, we want to talk with that special person and get to know him/her better...the way he/she does things and his/her life values. We look forward to getting to know the other person at a more intimate level. And, that's good, necessary, and godly, too.

Third, *believers* also have an inner desire to do all the above *according to God's will*. This desire isn't physical, it's moral and spiritual, and comes from both our conscience and our relationship with God. So, God wants us to get to know someone well before marriage, that only makes sense. But, we must let sex be something to look forward to within the boundaries of marriage. Build a godly reputation and date someone who has the same, while continuing to respect Biblical values and advice along the way.

Remember: it's incredibly *easy* to indulge in sexual pleasures outside of God's will, but it's also incredibly *difficult* to rid yourself of painful consequences. Many good relationships have been scared by getting too familiar physically before marriage, even if marriage eventually brings a couple together. So, learn to act upon your convictions, not your inclinations!

114

Surprise!

It was just a few days before Christmas and the last day of school before vacation. I was with some of my senior high friends walking down the hallway, when one of the "cool" kids, I'll call him Dave, stopped me after class.

"Hey, Ed, what's happenin'. Are you doing anything special for Christmas this year?" I didn't hang around with Dave's crowd too much, but he was a pretty good guy, President of the class and friendly enough.

"Naw. Just gonna lay low. Visiting some relatives like we usually do, I guess."

"Bummer. Sitting around and trying to make conversation, when you'd rather be home, right?"

"Yeah, mostly...but, I usually have an okay time with my cousin. We're both into sports and stuff."

Dave and his friends were known as the popular crowd, being team football and basketball players and such. The girls they dated and hung around with were usually the most attractive as well.

"Listen, how about coming out to my Christmas party next Tuesday night? Nothin' fancy, just some music and food. Come on out, if you can, okay?"

I was surprised, frankly, because I usually didn't get such invitations. But, I said yes, thinking it would be different. And, wow...was it!

Tuesday evening came along, and I headed over to Dave's house with another friend, Dennis, who was also invited. We knocked and were greeted by Dave, who led us to the basement/rec room, where the Christmas party was already in motion. There was a short flight of stairs, and my friend went down first. I noticed that there was a girl at each of the first three descending steps to greet us, thinking to myself, "Okay, different...I guess we're supposed to smile and shake hands on the way down."

Well, each girl tightly embraced us on the way down, and then each girl kissed us...I mean *really* kissed each of us." I thought I had drowned and was getting mouth-to-mouth resuscitation. One girl explored more parts of my mouth than my Dentist!

One of the girls, Diane, was Dave's girlfriend, and the other two I knew fairly well at school. Without even focusing upon the morality of it all, I'd never actually kissed a girl before this anyway, so I was somewhat dazed by this "close encounter" with the opposite sex. When I finally stepped into the basement, I tried to remain unsurprised and "cool" with everyone, but it wasn't easy.

Everything else was normal, however. Christmas type decorations hung on the walls, and there was music, some dancing, a lot of conversation and lots of food. After getting control of my emotions, I started making conversation with everyone I knew there. We only stayed for about an hour, because, again, this wasn't really my kind of crowd. The interests, the conversation, the language....the kissing....everything just told me to remove myself. And, so I did, thanking Dave for his genuine kindness, of course, for inviting me.

Life Lessons

This experience in today's social environments would be seen as just naïve, for sure. However, it's not that a country boy like myself was dead to understanding things about life and sex. I was just raised to respect guidelines for right & wrong and better & best in these matters. And, as a Christian, I also realized that it is essentially "hands off" until marriage. Unfortunately, in today's world and its non-Christian attitudes, people are expected.... even encouraged, not just to touch, but to guiltlessly "take the car out for a demo drive."

The problem with this anti-Biblical thinking is that God *has not* given us this freedom, guilt *is real,* and it *will impact our lives*...either now or later. I understand that a kiss is not necessarily the same thing as immorality, but it can be a significant enticement towards it.

The most common word for immorality in the Bible, by the way, is "pornea," from which we get the word pornographic. It means sexual indulgence of any kind outside of marriage. Certainly, we don't have to be afraid of a *simple* kiss, holding hands affectionately or a gentle, non-enticing hug...*in most cases.* But, all of us need to have "spiritual common sense" and avoid situations that can easily erode our spiritual convictions.

> *"It is God's will that you should avoid sexual immorality; that each of you should learn to control his own body in a way that is holy and honorable, not in passionate lust like (those)...who do not know God."* (I Thess. 4:3-5 NIV)

Please remember that *actions have consequences.* If you loosen the reigns too much, that horse just wants to jump out of the coral, and, frankly, that's absolutely normal. God created us to enjoy sexual pleasure, but not apart from HIS guidelines, whether or not our friends, high school counselor, school literature, or society's standards agree. Cut corners here and you can have disastrous effects, so watch the freedom you give yourself!

Ask Dave. Only a couple of months later, I noticed that he and his girlfriend, Diane, were not in class anymore. I discovered that he left school without graduating, and took a job somewhere in town, while his girlfriend (and now fiancé) was temporarily away. Can you guess why? Life choices, particularly in this area, really count! Please...choose wisely.

The College Years

College brought many experiences that tested the fiber of this cabin and country raised young man. The days of cabin living and teenage fun were still etched in my mind, of course. But, college presented new challenges for me to either uphold or reject godly values. Some experiences were funny, some difficult to revisit, but all necessary for God to move me toward spiritual maturity. I hope you will enjoy and profit from them, too.

Campus Life

"Gosh...eight hours!" I stretched and yawned while we exited the car. My parents dropped off Kathy, her friend Kathy, and myself for our first day at college in September. It was a long trip from Connecticut to Houghton College in upstate New York.

The campus was quite beautiful, particularly in those colorful late summer and early fall months. It was orientation day and the campus was alive with new students being dropped off by their parents. Most of the upperclassmen hadn't yet arrived, but they'd be coming in the next few days. We visited the student center and cafeteria, the dorms where we'd be staying and then just walked along the "quad." That was the grassy area at the center of the campus. We signed in as new students at the admin building and then grabbed something to eat.

My parents stayed until late afternoon, then left for the long journey home, getting there well after midnight. For most of the other trips home, we'd try to catch a standby flight, or hitch a ride with a student, who had a car and was going in our direction.

Later that week, after all the upperclassmen had arrived, there was one day of "hazing" allowed, where these returning students could ask the new students to do some really crazy things. We'd laugh as we saw other freshmen forced to do push-ups, hop on one foot, or stand up and sing something at lunch. Sometimes it went too far, however. I recall one kid actually hurting himself trying to do some crazy thing asked of him. The practice was outlawed the next year, I believe.

Houghton was situated 60 miles outside of Buffalo, New York in the country landscape of Allegheny County. So, there wasn't a

119

whole lot of trouble you could get into, frankly. It was a tiny rural town, which you'd miss driving through if you hiccupped! Main street had a pizza place, a small country store, a gas station.... that's about all!

College life was quite different...no one was there to tell you to get to class on time or get your homework done. No one watched over the types of friends you hung with, the books you read or the places you went to. However, there was another small town about 5 miles away, which was a bit larger than Houghton. It had a movie theater in it, which only sat about 75 people. Since, Houghton was a very conservative Christian school at the time, each student had to *sign a pledge* stating that he or she would not play cards, watch television, drink alcoholic beverages, smoke or go to the movies.

Now, I didn't smoke, drink or use drugs, but I did go to movies on occasion. Nevertheless, I had still signed the form. As time went by, there were a couple of movies that came out, which I wanted to see. I found out that most kids still took in a movie once in a while, so I went with them. One of the kids shouted out in the theater, "Hey...how many kids are here from Houghton...raise your hands!" Everyone laughed as the place was generously populated with Houghton students (regularly, I might add).

However, I went home feeling somewhat guilty. Yes, the college's pledge was somewhat immature, but I still signed the thing, so I was wrong and knew it. Everyone there knew it, but most of us chose to let it slide, unfortunately, in the months ahead.

Sundays at Houghton were really slow, for another school policy kept everything closed on campus, and the local stores were closed, too. You'd go to church Sunday morning and, perhaps, at night, too. But, during the day even sports were frowned upon. It was quite a switch, indeed, even from upbringing I had known.

One thing that truly annoyed me, however, was the closing of the music hall on Sundays, where people practiced their instruments, if they were involved in music programs like band, orchestra, etc. Now, I was used to practicing 2-3 hours a day in order to maintain a strong embouchure for playing the trumpet. Going a day without practice would genuinely compromise me for a couple of days or so, particularly since I was called to play in churches throughout the area on occasion. Now, practicing on Sunday wasn't against the rules, but the school didn't allow anyone to use the buildings on Sundays...so the result was the same.

In this area, I thought about how to deal with this unusual issue and not offend anyone at the same time. I discovered an old barn across the road and away from the campus. I'd bring the trumpet over there on Sundays just for an hour or so and play to the cows and trees. The barn's hay stacks, stalls and creaky wooden sides contained the sound fairly well. I don't think anyone was ever actually bothered by my long tones, scales and musical solos (though occasional "moos" did protest my high notes!). In this case, then, I *kept* the rules, but also met my own needs as well. I never talked to the Dean about it...or was asked to explain my actions. So, I guess my creativity passed spiritual muster.

Life Lessons

It's not always easy to be honest and above board, but it's the only choice to make. Just because most of the students at my college did not keep the rules 100%, didn't mean that I could break them, too. For the Christian, honesty and keeping your word are two principles that are never up for negotiation.

We all want certain things, but sometimes organizational rules at church, work or school won't allow us any personal freedoms. In such situations, it doesn't necessarily mean the rules *or* our opinions are right. Nevertheless, what *is* right in such situations is respecting the authority we have pledged ourselves to obey.

I'm glad that I stood up for an acceptable way to solve the Sunday practicing question. But, looking back, I'm sad to think that I didn't exercise personal restraint in the movie issue. Perhaps I could have had my parents intercede, asking the school to give some "elbow room" to students who wanted to attend, but who had minor disagreements. But, that rarely works, for organizations usually demand uniformity. The clear choice would have been to personally "man up" and avoid the areas involved in the pledge…or…leave and attend another college. Sin, and dishonesty in particular, is cunning and cuts moral corners any way it can. So, God instructs us to be very wise in dealing with it.

"…be shrewd as serpents and innocent as doves."
(Matthew 10:16)

The "Man" With The Brown Paper Bag

"I hope we're doing the right thing," Kathy asked me, as we arrived at Buffalo airport at 4:30 pm. An upperclassman at Houghton College was kind enough to drop us off at the airport.

"Don't worry, I've got it covered," I assured Kathy. "My friend, Rich, will meet us at 7:30 pm at LaGuardia Airport. What can go wrong?"

It was a cool October night in 1967. We were on a surprise visit to our parents living an hour outside New York City, our flight destination. We thanked our friend and hurried into the busy terminal.

"By the way, Ed, how much money do we have?"

"Oh, about five bucks for a coke or somethin'…should be enough." Kathy was silent.

Stand-by always worked before, but people were jamming the terminal today. At the gate, however, some unwanted words came over the loudspeaker.

"Sorry, but those waiting on stand-by can't board this flight. We'll try getting you on the 7 pm flight, if possible."

"If possible?" I looked at Kathy and frowned…we had no way back to the college (there were no cell phones at that time, either).

We hung around, using up our five dollars quickly. We returned to the boarding area amidst crying kids and weary travelers, all hustling around and hoping this 7 pm flight would take off without a hitch. I looked at the flight times and gasped. *This* flight was going to the *Newark* airport…22 miles *away* from LaGuardia!

"You're kidding," I quipped to the attendant. She responded firmly, "Do I look like I'm kidding?" I decided not to show my displeasure further and boarded the plane.

We landed in Newark at 8:15 pm. Next, we needed to cross town and find Rich, so we checked out rental cars. Hertz informed me that an 18 year old without a credit card was going nowhere. So, we just wandered the terminal, hoping for a miracle, I guess.

We stepped outside and reviewed our situation. Someone nearby overheard us discussing it and surprisingly offered us a few dollars in change. We couldn't believe it, but eagerly grabbed the money. He suggested we take a bus to the nearest subway and then head for the other airport, which we did.

The bus took us to a subway station, where we next boarded a train. Feeling overwhelmed, we prayed that God would get us out of this mess...and keep us from getting *mugged!* The crowded, rickety subway car was unnerving, so we talked about other things. One guy sitting next to us wearing a leather jacket and holding a brown paper bag, offered to help us.

"Listen....get off three stops *after* me. There's a bus stop on the street above, which will get you to the airport." We breathed a bit easier and followed his advice.

Three stops later at 10 pm, we finally emerging onto a dark, deserted side street in Queens...alone and scared. The silence was interrupted by a noisy crowd carrying flaming torches, trailed by a police car. Apparently, some sort of freedom march was passing by. I ran over and knocked on the window of the cruiser. The annoyed cop simply cracked the window slightly, scowled, and said, "Get lost, kid."

I was angry and disheartened at the same time, but returned to Kathy. What should we do?

I had her sit on her suitcase by the bus stop, while I wandered up a dark side-street for help. Looking to my right, I spotted an approaching man carrying a brown paper bag. I called out to him, realizing that it was the *same guy on the train, who got off miles before.* How could this be?

He walked over, smiling, and handed me $10 for a bus he said would be coming soon...then left into the night. I stood there relieved, but shocked, and glanced at Kathy in the distance. I ran back to her and excitedly explained what had happened....*as a bus turned the corner.* We climbed aboard and later found Rich, still faithfully waiting for us after 4 hours. *Amazing!* Two naive college freshmen had been visited by a heavenly messenger wearing a leather jacket...*and carrying a brown paper bag.*

Life Lessons

Kathy and I are convinced that we met an angel that day, perhaps a personally designated one...a "guardian angel." We'll never know for sure until we get to heaven, but I look forward to finding that out. Hebrews 13, verse 2 says:

> *"Do not forget to entertain strangers, for by so doing some people have entertained angels without knowing it."* NIV

I think people unfortunately try to find angels or even demons, "around every bush," as someone has quipped. But, such spiritual beings can't be everywhere at the same time, though the Bible does speak of legions of angels being at God's disposal.

Remember the angel who tried to help George Bailey in the movie, "It's A Wonderful Life?" In real life, however, the Bible doesn't encourage us to seek an angel's assistance or to pray to one of them for special intercession. But, they are busy doing God's purposes, and that sometimes means they are in our lives *personally* for a particular reason. How far that goes, I guess we'll have to wait for heaven for all the details.

Until then, let's be sensible...angels aren't really accessible for us upon demand. Though, perhaps I should have asked "our" angel, *"Hey...you know, a hundred bucks would go a lot further for me, bub!* Well, on second thought, maybe that wouldn't have gone over so well, either!"

The Sleep Out

"This is ridiculous," announced my roommate, and I responded with equal conviction.

"No kidding. Since when is *this* part of the gym program!"

We were walking up a long, gravel road toward the woods and away from the campus. It was now October, and the air was very cool and windy, giving us an early taste of the approaching winter. Each of us was carrying a make-shift bedroll and was still dressed in fall type clothing. Unfortunately, as part of the Houghton commitment to its gym program, the Coach was taking our class of 20 guys into the hills for an overnight sleep-over. Why anyone would want to sleep out in the woods in 40 degree weather without at least having a sufficient sleeping bag for the occasion...I simply don't know. But, it was part of the program in order to teach us "survival skills."

Okay, survival stuff is kind of exciting, particularly if you're watching "Bear Grylls" or some other survival dude on television. But, college kids with sneakers, just school-type clothing and no gloves or hiking outer wear....well, that's just crazy. I did notice, by the way, that the coach had on the appropriate survival duds for the occasion! This particular gym experience, however, wasn't in the literature and was announced quickly, so most all of us just had to endure it half-prepared.

It was now about 8 pm. Having arrived at a pre-selected spot, we broke up in two's and were told to find a comfortable spot to start a campfire for some warmth through the night. We had no tents, either, just our dorm blankets and pillows. Fortunately, we had already eaten dinner, but we did stow away some chips and candy, though technically not "part of the real experience." Most of us took over an hour to dig out some sort of shelter. When darkness arrived, all of us just wanted to hit the sack and pray that tomorrow would come quickly. But, darkness around here was what some call "pitch black," almost zero light without a moon.

Now, let me be more descriptive about our spot in the woods. First, it was on a slight hill with uneven mounds of leaves and fallen branches scattered all around. If it rained, we would have been two bodies in a flood of muddy water careening down the hill out of control! The weather was so cold, stray snowflakes fell on our faces as we rested on our pillows, which, of course, also invited every bug to nest there with us as well. The blanket I had brought to college was the only one I had and was not made for outdoor events. It was not very large nor was it made of wool, and it seemed to keep pulling itself off me through the night. At one point, I got so angry at it, I barked, "Stop pulling away, will ya!" Immediately, I thought I heard it reply, "Speak to yourself, I'm covering up, too!" (perhaps I was delirious).

Well, between the owls hooting, squirrels scurrying and crickets squeaking, the morning sun did *not* come quickly over the horizon. In fact, it was a cold, overcast and foggy morning. My roommate and I heard the coach blow the "rise and shine" whistle, but groaned and just turned over.

"Hey, troops...get up," he shouted. "It's a great day that the Lord has made!" I considered the possibility that the Lord had made somewhat of a mistake on this particular day and opened my mouth to inform the coach about it. However, his annoying, positive attitude convinced me otherwise. So, we groggily got up, reassembled ourselves and returned to our dorms, after which we cleaned up and went to class (right!).

I really enjoy watching the survival type shows on the Discovery channel. Because of this, I'm pretty sure I could start a fire to keep warm, prepare a dry bed of branches to sleep on and devise a make-shift shelter to keep me out of the cold and wind.

I've never been in a true survival situation, where my life might be hanging in the balance of making wise decisions and safe precautions. But, I have encountered spiritual survival situations in my life, where my spiritual life might rightly be considered "on the line." Those were times (as a believer) where I was not walking in right relationship with God. I had, indeed, slipped into significant sin. If God had not stepped into those difficulties and/or disasters, my life would have turned out quite different. I'm not one to believe that my salvation would have truly been in jeopardy, but it might have been a close call!

As Christians, we're in a spiritual survival situation to some degree, until we get to heaven. But, when we stray from the daily closeness we've been accustomed to in the Lord, we can expect to feel significant discomfort and stress. Such unpreparedness also exposes us to the cold breezes of temptation, where we feel alone and susceptible to sin. There, his love appears to us as just faint whispers in the breeze instead of warm intimacy with Jesus.

So, my advice is to always think ahead and be prepared to boldly face whatever comes your way. Spiritual survival depends upon many things, but one thing is a key part of it:

> *"Watch and pray so that you will not fall into temptation. The spirit is willing, but the body is weak."* (Matt. 26:41 NIV)

Thank God that we can survive any onslaught of temptation in our lives by his readily available mercy and grace. But, when we're prepared, survival can be fairly enjoyable, even when facing the challenges of a cold, lonely night camping out in a dark forest.

Demonic Curiosity

It was a boring night with nothing to do, so a few of the guys in the dorm came into our room just to "shoot the breeze." One thing led to another, and one of them said, "Hey, I've got a Ouija Board, let's play a game or two!"

"Wait a minute," one of the guys responded, "I've heard that's not something we ought to mess with. It opens the door to demons."

"Oh, please!" someone replied. "Come on, don't be a wimp... it's just a game." So, we all decided, stupidly I might add, to get the game and play.

Soon we were deep into it, everyone moving their fingers with subconscious coordination to spell out words and messages. I had never played it before, so I was quite skeptical. But, because of its reputation, all of us wanted to give it a try. So, here we were, five Christian college kids on a dark winter night near midnight playing with something most believers think can be a very real channel for demonic influence.

We laughed at some of the crazy "revelations" the board spelled out to us, wondering how it could know things about each of us. Most seemed reasonably harmless, until I asked it to tell me the middle name of the girl God wants me to marry. We moved the pointer slowly, trying to feel the letters it wanted us to go to, and it spelled out the first few letters of my girlfriend's name at the time. I was a bit nervous, so I backed off the pointer and let the others "feel moved" by their fingers. Without me, it actually finished spelling out her middle name! I sat back in astonishment.

"Hey....not one of you knew that. How did it...." I didn't finish the sentence, because of its implications.

"That's it," someone said, "I'm not messing with that thing anymore, that's for sure!" And, we never did again.

Life Lessons

There's a whole lot we don't understand about the spirit world. Halloween, for instance, is mostly just fooling around stuff, though there are groups of people who take its history for real and actually worship Satan. But, dressing up and saying "trick or treat" for candy really isn't going to conjure up any demons, I'm sure.

However, there is a point at which people can step over the line and easily make contact with demonic entities. One of them, I'm convinced, is the Ouija Board game. Most often it's probably just subconscious antics, but I believe that there can be times when it becomes a doorway to evil entities. It's been proven, of course, that people can move the pointer subconsciously to say things they already know. But, as anyone *also* knows who's played it, there's a significant amount of information revealed at times, which could not possibly be known....like my girlfriend's middle name.

So, here's a tip about demons and evil spirits. They can "reach out" to hurting individuals at vulnerable times in their lives, e.g. child abuse, drug involvement, sexual promiscuity, etc. Still, not every situation invites a demonic presence, for demons aren't omnipresent (existing everywhere). But, evil situations sometimes *can* bring us into contact with their presence in such a way that we fall under their influence, if we foolishly reach out for contact.

I'm not an expert in all this....and, I don't want to be, but it's nothing to fool around with. King Saul sought out the spirit world by going to a witch, something he was told not to do. He was definitely enamored by these things, because even before this, he was receptive to an evil spirit, which God allowed to happen, because of his spiritually disobedient lifestyle. The result was personal torment, suffering, and murderous behaviors. The Bible is clear on this:

> *"Let no one be found among you who...practices divination or sorcery, interprets omens, engages in witchcraft, or cast spells, or who is a medium or spiritist or who consults the dead. Anyone who does these things is detestable to the Lord."* (Deut. 18:10, 11 NIV)

But, what about just playing games and not contacting demons by choice? That's a very questionable door that we just shouldn't open, because of the inherent danger in it. One doesn't play with electricity...why play with occultic-focused games?

My youth director once asked me an important question in this context. If I was driving down a slippery narrow mountain road, would I try to hug the inside or try to go as fast as I could along the *edge* of the 500 foot drop? The answer was obvious: "Stay as far away as possible." Scripture wisely warns us about all this:

> *"...he who seeks evil, evil will come to him."* (Pr. 11:27b)

So, don't hug dangerous spiritual roads in your life, okay. They can really be a disaster, if you lose control. By the way, as is often the case with an Ouija Board, it lied about that middle name!

Halloween Surprise

"Please be advised that a prisoner, incarcerated for assault as well as bomb construction, has escaped. Although the entire Cheshire police force is on alert, the governor has asked local authorities to warn all businesses and citizens of this imminent danger. Do not try to apprehend nor accept any strange packages from unknown people. Notify the  local authorities immediately, if you have reason to suspect you have encountered this individual. Thank you."*

Now, I ask you, "Isn't that a serious situation of which one should take notice? Wouldn't you be very suspicious of anyone creeping in the dark around your house at night?" If you agree, then I would have fooled you as well.

You see, that first fall at college seemed unending. All of us freshmen could hardly wait to get back home at Thanksgiving time and see everyone. At the time, I was casually dating a high school senior, who still went to the church youth group. It was Halloween time, and I was figuring a way to surprise her by coming home for a weekend visit on Halloween. A friend let me borrow his car, so I scooted out early in the day for the 7 hour trip home from college. When I arrived in the area, I called another friend at my home church and asked him to call up the girl's father around 5 pm and convincingly read the announcement above.

Well, it worked fantastically! It was dark when I arrived that night, but I parked the car up the street. Grabbing a cardboard box about the size of a computer from the back seat, I stuffed a ticking clock inside, set the alarm to go off in ten minutes, then I sealed it with tape. So far…so good.

I got out of the vehicle and crept down the dark, country road to my girlfriend's house. Looking around from my spot in the bushes by the road and seeing no one, I got up and silently approached the porch. I laid the box down by the door, knocked and then scrammed back to my spot behind the bushes to observe what would happen next. My girlfriend opened the door, looked down at the box, and brought it into the house. She called her father over to see the package, just about the time the alarm went off.

"Get that outa here," he yelled, "It's a bomb!"

"Her father grabbed a nearby broom from behind the door and shoved the package off the porch. As he slammed the door, you could hear all kinds of commotion going on inside. My plan had worked….however, what was I to do now? I mean, they were really scared. What if they called the police?

I quickly ran up to the door, knocked and was greeted with a hug from my girlfriend, who as completely taken in. Of course, everyone put two and two together quickly, and realized that it was just a surprise visit gag. Her mother was fine with it, laughing and rewarding me with some chocolate pie and ice cream. *However, I don't remember her father being quite as cordial!*

Life Lessons

In today's world, such shenanigans probably would have brought Homeland Security agents to the doorstep! My parents and everyone had no problem with it, once all was known. In fact, the friend I had to call in the fake warning was my home Pastor, who knew the family well and was in on the gag.

Perhaps you, too, are someone who likes to kid around like this with some of your friends, who would also enjoy doing the same to you. Consider, however, the following before you go overboard. Never be rude or crude in your jokes, verbally or otherwise, for the Lord is not pleased with vulgarity or insensitivity. Also, never have fun *at the expense* of someone else, such that the person becomes *seriously* embarrassed or deeply hurt. Fun is one thing, but hurting someone in an unkind way would never be acceptable. Scripture mentions the following guideline:

"Nor should there be obscenity, foolish talk or coarse joking, which are out of place..." (Eph. 5:4 NIV)

Overall, having fun with people you know and love is great, as long as you're always careful about how you do it. I did do an elaborate prank on someone later on in my adult life, and unfortunately opened up an intense fear within that person, of which I had no knowledge. Feelings of threat and excessive vulnerability resulted, which I never would have wanted to stir up from that person's past history. So....be careful *how* you fool around with folks and play jokes or pranks. You may be on the receiving end of something you really didn't expect.

Bad Choices

It's really challenging, when you go to a new school or start a new job and face a different environment with new people to get to know. One college friend, who we'll call Rob, was an affable Christian student, but very naive  regarding spiritual things. He was definitely a believer, but just not very knowledgeable or discerning, let's say.

We were on the 3rd floor of Wood Hall at Gordon College, where I later transferred from Houghton. One night, I remember seeing a bunch of guys in the room across from Rob's room. They were all quietly gathered around each other and watching something in a guarded way. I stepped into the room and walked over to see what was holding their attention so well. Peering over the shoulder of one of the guys, I saw why they were so mesmerized. They were looking at some pornographic magazines supplied by a returning upper-classman, who we'll call John.

I don't think I'd ever even seen a Playboy before, let alone this type of stuff. So, I was startled and embarrassed, frankly, by what I saw in front of me. Nevertheless, all of us were glued to what was pictured before our eyes.

"Hey," said one the guys, "let's go, before a monitor comes by. Anyway, we shouldn't be doing this."

"Awe, you guys need to know what's out there in the real world," John countered. "You think God doesn't know what sex is all about? Come on, get real! How can you talk about God with somebody, if you don't know what the world is really like?"

After that outstanding display of spiritual "insight," I and a few others recognized such stupidity and left…but, not everyone did so. Rob was one of those who stayed, but he was unprepared to face this sort of temptation, more so than the rest of us.

Over the months ahead, Rob found himself "mentored" by John and his skewed, carnal coaching. John had a car, so he would often take Rob and others downtown to see triple X movies, for instance, or to other porn stores. He did this all in the name of gaining what he referred to as "grown-up spirituality," where such exposure, according to him, *would help one better understand non-believers and their thinking.*"

Well, he helped Rob, all right. Rob ended up getting involved in deeper sexual sins, eventually ending up with emotional problems and having to leave school. I don't know what happened to him from there on, but I'm sure his life would never be the same, due primarily because of the "spiritual insights" he had encountered in that 3rd floor "Christian" porn shop.

Life Lessons

I'd like to talk for a bit about relationship choices. Rob lacked common sense and hung around with someone he shouldn't have. Because of this, he was simply sucked into a sewer of sinful activities, resulting in a devastating downward spiral into disaster.

But, there are all kinds of people – younger or older - whose misguided relationships drag them into circumstances that overwhelm their spiritual stamina and strength. To use another example, how many people you know have gotten deep into drugs or alcohol, who thought that a "little" experimentation wouldn't hurt. Yet, if they had exercised even a "little" bit of caution and wisdom, they wouldn't have fallen into its grip.

But, that grip of desire wasn't just from sex or drugs alone, *it came about because of bad relationship choices.* We should be cautious about whom we listen to and hang around with. Try to look beyond someone's personality, no matter how funny, cordial or charming they may be. Learn to think beyond the shallow ideas people may throw at you to justify what you know to be sin and avoid intimate or unnecessary contact with such people. Kindly challenge their misguided, indulgent or rebellious thinking when you can, but stay at a distance relationally. Why? Their witness and influence over you might be more effective than yours toward them. Remember, Scripture wisely instructs us:

> *"Do not be misled: "Bad company corrupts good character."* (I Cor. 15:33 NIV)

So, build your convictions upon God's Word and then live your life confidently upon those convictions. Bad choices can be devastating...just ask Rob.

Have Trumpet...Will Travel

"You're in, Ed!" Stan looked at me with enthusiastic approval.

"Well...alright!" I returned, and then began asking all kinds of detailed questions about where to meet next fall.

I had just tried out and won a place on tour with a Christian musical group called the Spurrlows. Each year this semi-professional group of mostly college age, Christian musicians came through the Buffalo area. Stan was lead trombone and head writer for the touring musical group. He liked what I could do with the trumpet and invited me to tour with them around the country in the coming year.

The Spurrlows group toured during the school year, working for Chrysler Corporation during the day, then performed pop music concerts in high schools at night. Wrapped within the music was a message to the teenagers about safe driver education. At night and on weekends, the group put on Christian concerts in churches and concert halls across the country...our main purpose, of course. I was selected to join them in the fall, as lead trumpet in an ensemble of 12 musicians and a chorus of 15.

The school year seemed to go quickly, and I joined the group in Spring Arbor, Michigan for their August music camp lasting six weeks. We practiced the new scores of music and learned all the choreography, then began our year-long tour across the nation!

- - - - - - - - - - - - - - - - - -

"Beautiful day," I mumbled to myself as I walked along the empty sidewalk in downtown Chicago at 6 am. It was a clear and sunny morning, and I had left the hotel early to grab a quick breakfast before meeting the group at the assigned time. Sometimes we'd stay in hotels, while at other times we'd stay in the homes of people at our church concerts. This particular time we stayed at a hotel in a not-so-good area of the city to save money, though the hotel itself was fine. We had to meet at 6:45 am and then travel an hour or so to our first gig (a high school assembly concert). We usually performed 3 or 4 of these each day and traveled a hundred miles or so each day as well.

As I stepped out of the downtown hotel, I didn't think much about my location. But, as I walked along, I noticed a man coming from the other way toward me, wearing in a long, dark trench coat.

"That's odd," I thought, for it really wasn't that cold out.

He stopped about 15 feet away and stared at me, but I kept walking toward him. Suddenly, he he pulled out a switch blade from his pocket and turned menacingly toward me, just as I was approaching him. I was obviously startled and scared, but I gritted my teeth and spontaneously shouted into his face, "Don't you dare!" And...I kept walking.

I must have really shocked *him,* for he just stood there watching me pass by! I looked back at him after about ten feet or so, and he was still staring at me with a look of disbelief on his face.

Life Lessons

Seriously, I couldn't believe that I had been set up to be robbed, perhaps even killed, but God had instead been merciful and protected me. The lesson I learned from the above situation was to "think better." Casually taking a walk alone in a remote part of town is *not* a sensible thing to do, particularly when you're nineteen years old, naïve and on a side street in Chicago at 6 in the morning! Proverbs 14:15 offers some wise counsel in this regard:

"The naïve believes everything, but the sensible man considers his steps."

God obviously stepped in to protect this naïve, former cabin-dwelling country boy to real world dangers. But, God prefers, I believe, that we learn how to make sensible choices in life situations that challenge us. We've been given a brain to use and shouldn't *expect* supernatural intervention at every turn in life (though I'm happy to say that he does provide such on occasion!).

Have you heard the phrase, "He's so heavenly-minded he's no earthly-good?" There's a lot of pain coming to someone who resembles that description, for the learning process can be hard on such a person. That's why I like the book of Proverbs so much, it's full of real life stuff to help me along in my Christian walk. All of us should be heavenly-minded, of course, but we should also be sensitive to the practical necessities and responsibilities of life. As a well-known speaker once said to a group of Christian teenagers at a church rally:

"So, you want to be a powerful and influential leader for God some day? Great...but, let me ask you an important question. 'Did you make your bed this morning?'"

Think about that. It's great to desire to serve God in big ways, but we've got to be responsible to Him in the little things first.

Earthly things - that which is necessary, daily, sensible and practical - is a responsibility for everyone, including believers. There's a world of potential danger out there, ready to slice into you with evil intentions, just like that street bum. Most often, however, dangerous situations can be avoided and/or diffused, if we simply use the brain God gave to each of us. God allowed my bluff to work that morning in Chicago, but he could have had me learn such wisdom the hard way, instead. I'll choose door number one, thank you!

Lessons On Humility

"Going for the "high F" at the
end?" Terry asked me. Terry was a
humble guy and also played trumpet
in our musical troupe. His kindness
and gentle spirit was appreciated by
all members of the band and chorus,

and he eventually became a successful song writer for Disney.
Unfortunately, at the time, I was not so humble, when it came to
playing the trumpet.

"Sure…why not. My chops feel great." And, at the end of that
musical number, I hit a pretty good high note.

All through high school I had won awards and played in various
bands and orchestras around Connecticut and was used to seeking
and getting praise. At every concert with the Spurrlows, I received
plenty of accolades by playing a trumpet solo, sometimes in front
of a whole lot of people.   At camp, the leaders even showed us
how to do things for "show," like straining for a high note, when
you're really not.

"It looks great and people clap all the more, because they think
you're accomplishing something beyond what someone else can
do," they would say. It's just "showmanship." Okay, but
showmanship without humility never pleases the Lord.

Well, by the end of the year God taught me a lot about pride
and why I needed to personally deal with it. The first experience
was in Texas, where the other two trumpet players and I were
warming up in an empty classroom before our first assembly of the
day. It was about 8am, and we heard music coming from the band

141

room nearby, so we checked it out. Inside, the high school jazz band was just finishing their practicing period….and they sounded great (we later learned they were nationally known themselves). One of the high school students asked us to sit in with their trumpet section, I'm not sure why, but probably just to show off. The other two guys declined, not wanting to possibly embarrass themselves in front of another player. Not me, of course, for I was ready to show the world how good I was, right?

They started the number, and suddenly these younger, high school trumpet players were screeching out high "G's" and "double C's" that I could only dream of hitting. Yes, they lacked the professional ability to do what we did every day, but they still sounded great. So, I just briefly played one chart as written, then excused myself, for our concert was going to start soon anyway.

As I was walking down the hall to the auditorium, Terry sarcastically, but rightfully, asked me, "Well, did you get what you wanted?" I ignored the comment, and continued down the hall toward the auditorium to set up for our assembly. But, in my own mind, I knew what he was saying. "You could have embarrassed all of us, trying to show off like that." And, he was right.

Later on, we traveled to another Texas town for more concerts, then on to a church for a two hour Christian concert. That night, as I lay in a hotel bed, my mind was racing. Why did I have to feel like I had to show everyone how good I was?

I can recall another experience as a high school sophomore, after winning a place in the Connecticut Allstate Orchestra as lead trumpet player. We played a symphony by composer, Jean Sibelius. It was long and had a very, very quiet part in the middle of it, where I had to play a short, four note solo. The audience of 2000 sat attentively to this special concert, which was being recorded, and which highlighted the best musical students in the state.

"Okay, here comes my part," I said to myself. Everything was so quiet you could hear a whisper on stage, while the violins played softly in the background. I put my mouthpiece to my lips and...promptly *flubbed the last note.* I couldn't believe it! My mistake, though slight, was now recorded for the whole world to hear! Unfortunately, that humbling experience still didn't keep me from doing what I did in that Texas high school band 4 years later.

The last battle I faced with my inflated desire to "pat myself on the back" was at the end of the tour with the Spurrlows. At the Christmas break, when we all went home for two weeks, I hardly practiced...to my shame, frankly. I was just hanging around and doing nothing but enjoying the time off. Because of this, when I went back and started playing 4 or 5 concerts a day, I foolishly shifted the mouthpiece all around just to be able to play. Well, it threw my embouchure off and weakened my "chops" so much I had to give over my solo spot to Terry (who did a great job for the remainder of the year). I maintained my position as lead trumpet, as well as most of my technical ability, but I had so destroyed my embouchure that I never again played with the capability or the endurance I once had known. It was a very costly lesson.

Life Lesson

We all make mistakes, that's for sure. God understands this, of course, and tries to warn us in his Word so we can avoid the most obvious ones. And, a common one is pride.

My trumpet skill was very good, but I thought I was good enough to take a Christmas holiday and not practice at all, just sit back and enjoy. How foolish, but pride and ego do that to us, urging us to make decisions that bring unforeseen or unnecessary results. In my case, that "holiday" decision was disastrous. The rest of the year I was quite miserable, unable to perform the way I wanted and was expected to do.

What talents has God given to you to use? Are you gifted in some skill that can earn you a good living later on? Are you well known for some creative or musical ability? What is your spiritual talent or gift bank, and do you know what God has specifically given you to use for his glory?

When it comes to our abilities, each one of us has both strengths and weaknesses. Try to identify them clearly to yourself and your future will be much easier to understand, particularly as you search for God's will regarding a career. In the spiritual realm, God has also equipped you with certain definable abilities to use for his glory in the church.

> *"To each one is given the manifestation of the Spirit for the common good."* (I Cor. 12:7)

As you learn to define yourself in these areas and start planning for your future, be quick to stay humble and thankful to God for whatever he has given you. There are few things worse to see than a person whose talents make him or her "puffed up" and carrying around an exaggerated opinion of himself in front of others.

Looking back on it all, perhaps I wasn't proud to that extreme, but my pride did affect my ability to serve Christ fully. More performances than I would like to think about were spiritually "out of focus," while I reached for high notes and applause, instead of humbly serving my Savior. Because of that, I lost a lot of God's blessing over the years, both in ministry and in my career choices.

Even the overall group itself had to deal with the self-glory that would sometimes creep into our performances. These necessitated times of group confession and repentance, where we cleaned up our issues and put Christ back on the throne, where he belonged. A meaningful verse for me in this area was Isaiah 66:2b:

> *"But to this one I will look, to him who is humble and contrite of spirit, and who trembles at My word."*

Flashing Lights

"Man, this car really moves out," I said to the others in the car as I sped along the Arizona highway at 95 mph.

"You better believe it. This 440 gets about 375hp," came the reply from one of the guys in the back set of this new Dodge Charger. Our musical troupe traveled the country in six, new Chrysler vehicles, followed by a huge, 50 foot truck carrying all our staging, instruments, electronics and clothing. Normally, I didn't get a chance to drive the Charger, for it was driven by one of the leaders.

Now, I must explain that there were no speed limits at that time, when traveling in some of the western states on highways outside of the city limits. Sounds crazy today, but it was perfectly legal and acceptable then. You were on your own. The highways cutting through the Arizona desert or the low lands of Colorado were long and flat, safe for driving at a 100 mph or more...and many did.

We were heading for Phoenix, Arizona and were passing near the Grand Canyon in route to our evening concert. At one point, we exited the highway and stopped at one of those scenic overlooks along the way. We were dazzled by the gorgeous handiwork of God sculpting so many colorful rock formations along canyon rivers like the Colorado.

"Hey, we better get going, or we'll be late," cautioned George, another trumpet player in the group. So, we reluctantly pulled ourselves away from our scenic perch and continued the four hour trek.

We were running a bit late, so I increased the pace a bit by avoiding any more stops. Finally, we passed within the city limits of Phoenix, though I failed to notice the sign designating it so. Traffic was increasing, so I did drop the speed to about 85 mph.

Up ahead we spotted what looking like one of our cars pulled over to the side by a police cruiser with his lights flashing. As we got closer, we saw that we were right and began flashing our own lights at the driver, who had several other band members with him. He had passed us a half hour ago doing more than a 100 mph with everyone laughing at us as he sped by. So, it was now our turn.

We passed him with windows rolled down, honking our horn and waving wildly. The traffic cop didn't seem to mind us doing so, he just calmly wrote his ticket. We were laughing and joking around so much over it, we couldn't wait to get to our destination and rib them some more.

Unfortunately, I failed to see who had been following *me* a mile down the road. Yes, we had also missed the city limit sign, and…yup…there it was, a flashing red surprise in my rear view mirror! Another officer had been following us in an unmarked car and saw us mock out our friends. He never said a word about it, when handing out the ticket to me. But, he must have been laughing to himself like crazy!

Well, that was an expensive ticket, as I remember, but it was the *only* one I got for the whole year on tour. It was a memory which clearly remains etched in my mind to this day. All of the riders ridiculed the others that night, but the last and loudest laugh was *not* mine.

Life Lessons

Sometimes, it is a bit humorous the way some folks get themselves into trouble. But, there are also serious times when we're just cruising along in life, oblivious to our own spiritual responsibilities. Then, when trouble comes, the laugh is on us.

All of us make mistakes in many areas of life and get caught at it at times, but it's never a good thing to laugh at the misfortunes of someone else. Rather, it's a time to humbly look at ourselves and take stock of our *own* spirituality. Have we looked down on someone? Have we failed to recognize our own weaknesses in a similar area? Or, are we blinded by our own ego or position in life?

Spiritual blindness is not good, for it causes us to be *overly and unnecessarily* critical about *other* people's issues, while at the same time avoiding our own spiritual issues. It can also breed unkindness, prejudice and broken relationships, when we do so. As someone has quipped, "When you point your finger at someone else, you've got three fingers pointing back at yourself!"

That's why God commands us not to judge others, but to "remove the log" from our own eyes before trying to highlight someone else's sin.

> *"For in the same way you judge others, you will be judged, and with the measure you use, if will be measured to you."*
> (Matthew 7:2 NIV)

This makes special sense even when driving down an Arizona highway at 85 mph thinking you're the only one of significance on the road. Can you say…"Good afternoon, officer."

147

Circumstances

"What are we going to do?" I said to Stan, our troupe leader and head writer.

"Don't worry about it, Ed. We'll get someone from the local union to fill in for him for the night."

It was Friday night, we were in Miami, and we had a huge hall rented out for all the area churches to attend our concert. The problem was that our 2nd trumpet, George, was sick and we really needed him. So, the General Manager of the tour group made a call to the local musicians union. They sent out a guy to fill in for George, who was quite capable, as we found out. I was a member of the musician's union in Connecticut as a teenager and would sometimes get a call to fill in somewhere. You had to be able to sight read music well and also perform without much rehearsal.

The concert went along well. As I remember, the stage was a huge shell-like structure built out from the shoreline and separate from the seating. On the land side, there were probably seats for 1500 people, and tonight it was full. The night was moonlit and clear, and the crowd enjoyed our worship concert very much.

I was impressed with the union guy, and guessed that he had probably never attended a church or Christian concert before. "Did he even know the Gospel, or how to become a believer in Christ?" I asked myself.

As always, 2 or 3 members of the group would give testimonies at the end of the concert, and sometimes an altar call would take place. But, this night, with the physical layout being so different, we did not give people any opportunity to come forward. So, I asked the Lord to give me an opportunity to share Christ with this guy.

At the end, while we were putting our instruments back in the truck and heading back to the hotel, he asked if he could have a ride back to his home, which wasn't too far away, as it turned out. Immediately, I responded, "Absolutely....I'd be glad to do so." This was my chance, so I sought the Lord's leading, hoping this man would be receptive to the Gospel, when I shared it.

I didn't know my way around Miami too well, but within twenty minutes or so, we arrived at his house. I had been chatting with him about why we did these concerts, that we were believers and wanted to bring others to a saving knowledge of Christ.

"Would you be open to receiving Christ as your personal Savior right now?" I asked him respectfully, but compassionately. He responded affirmatively, so right there in the Spurrlow's car in front of the man's house, he asked Jesus to come into his life as Savior and Lord." I had grabbed some follow-up literature from the concert before and handed it to him, also encouraging him to seek out a godly and conservative church in the area. I informed my leadership, when I got back, so they could notify a local church to take the initiative and follow-up with him, if possible. So, it was one of those especially fantastic occasions, where God used someone...in this case myself...to step out of his comfort zone and be available for His purposes.

Life Lessons

I had someone tell me once that he thought I had a gift of evangelism. All of us, of course, have considered how God has gifted us so that we can appropriately involve ourselves in His work. However, as I considered his words and looked over my life, I came to the conclusion that there was really nothing "special" at all given to me in this specific area. Yes, I've led people to the Lord through the years, but I think that those experiences were simply *responsible choices* to follow God's leading. I've known some people, however, who were truly gifted in evangelism, and I'm certain that I don't model that capacity. But, God's Spirit, regardless of gifting, does ask us to follow his lead to share Christ with others as he opens up opportunities. Being responsible here is important, okay.

On the negative side, I also remember a time when a girl who I was dating shared with me that her uncle was in the hospital dying. I immediately expressed genuine concern for him, because she said he was not a believer. I then told her that I would try to visit him the next week, seeking an opportunity to share the Gospel with him. Well...I never did. I simply forgot.

Forgetting is sometimes a measuring stick for motivation. I was genuinely interested in visiting him, but not moved enough to put feet to my feelings. Frankly, none of us are ultimately responsible for anyone's salvation or loss of it, but I did fail in my responsibility to be used in that process with her uncle. It was a sad, but true lesson for me to learn, which has never left my mind.

How about you, are you looking for opportunities to share your faith with others who have a Christ-less future ahead of them? Will you look for ways to gently ask some simple, probing questions to see if someone might be open to the Gospel?

> "*...always be prepared to give an answer to everyone who asks you to give the reason for the hope that you have.*"
> (I Peter 3:15 NIV)

Back To College...And A Choice

It was a great year away, travelling as I did across this beautiful country. But, now it was fall, and I was back to real life, even though I was asked to stay on and travel with the group. Some did travel for repetitive  years, but it was tough on the families, because they would be traveling so much. As mentioned before, I returned to a different college, Gordon College, in the Boston area, from which I would eventually graduate with a degree in Psychology.

However, there was one last gig I did with the Spurrlows during the year I enrolled as a sophomore at Gordon. It so happened that I had committed myself to weekend involvement with the Gordon Ministry Team, which went out to local churches and put on small concerts of music and worship. One such event, an extended one, was planned for the coming Christmas vacation. It would be a week and a half of musical ministry through several states, which also served as a promotional vehicle for the college as well.

About two weeks before we were to leave on the Gordon College tour, I received a special invitation to play trumpet again for a week of concerts in Detroit with the Spurrlows (one of the trumpet players had to leave tour unexpectedly). My week would end by playing at their annual Christmas Concert in Detroit to a capacity crowd of over 10,000 thousand people. Of course, I had already committed myself to the Gordon College ministry team. So, what should I do? What would you have done?

I decided to go with the Spurrlows for a week of performances, citing that this was a unique and special opportunity to help the group with which I had traveled before. I thought it over, basing my decision upon the fact that my solo participation in the Gordon group was actually quite minor, and that it would not be missed.

However, the Dean saw it differently. He brought me into his office and explained that the Spurrlows opportunity was significant and very rewarding, one with which Gordon could not equal in any way. However, he continued by suggesting that a commitment made *is worth keeping,* particularly if it involves a commitment to God and a week of ministry. I had made a commitment, and he expected me to stay with it, though he could not force me do so. Nevertheless, my decision was to go to Detroit..

Life Lesson

Unfortunately, I later knew that I had made the *wrong* decision. I went off to Detroit and did have a great time performing with a group of talented, Christian young people from around the country. The concerts went fine, and the Christmas Concert was fabulous. But, when it was over and I was flying home for the holidays, I realized that the small, college tour group, ministering to a few churches, probably had more eternal results than a grandiose and recorded Christmas concert. While in Detroit, I didn't lead anyone to Christ, nor did the group, though we were on TV. I didn't get the chance to counsel anyone in their faith. But, of course, I did play trumpet before thousands. Do you see what I'm getting at? It was just entertainment (not necessarily bad, of course) with little spiritual or eternal impact.

The Gordon experience would have been smaller, for sure, but yielding a much greater impact for Christ. Worshipful music and testimonies would have impacted people in these churches, with perhaps someone more likely finding Christ as Savior and Lord. I definitely would have had opportunity to assist others in their walk with God, those who came forward at invitations. I also would have benefited myself, spiritually speaking, from all of the above. So, it was a poor and *selfish* decision, and it probably tarnished my reputation a bit with the college leadership. When considering similar decisions, consider the following:

- Are my priorities aligned with the Word of God?
- Am I thinking selfishly or compassionately?
- What is the most productive from an eternal perspective?
- What might be better and more pleasing to God?

Such questions are important to revisit, when trying to discern the will of God. We must try to think *beyond* the immediate and beyond the things that are only comfortable to us alone.

Scripture warns us that one day those who take the lead and serve God in more visible ways will be accountable for their actions:

> *"Let not many of you become teachers, my brethren, knowing that as such we will incur a stricter judgment."*
> (James 3:1)

In golf they say, "Putt for 'dough,' drive for show." They mean that hitting a ball a long way is quite an accomplishment and really impresses people, when they see it. However, though many top pros can't drive the farthest, they will win more games because they do well the thing less showy ... the *short iron* performance, especially putting. Such skill is seldom very ostentatious to behold, but it wins them more tournaments overall and brings in the big bucks! So, are you known as a spiritual driver or putter?

Studying, Statistics and Success

"I don't know if I've mentioned this before, but I wasn't really motivated in high school to study and get good grades. In the first cabin book, I shared how my father tried to turn that attitude around with an unfortunate slap across the face. That  was a wake-up call to me, but for the most part, I was never a "focused" student. I think that's because I didn't find something that "scratched where I itched," as they say. In other words, only in those classes that interested me would I get good grades.

Now, college enlarged that motivation somewhat. I chose Psychology as my major, because of its value for guys who wanted to go into ministry. But, I really didn't get super-excited about it, as I did, for instance, regarding Bible courses. I always did well in those, because of the joy I had in studying the Bible in my own personal walk with Christ. Still, I was probably just an average student, grade-wise. Let me share three classes that were downright annoying to me, okay (nothing personal to the prof's!).

One such class, which I thought would be interesting, was "Philosophy of Christianity." It was offered in the spring and seemed to be a helpful topic for a pre-seminary student to take. And, by coincidence, Kathy took the class as well.

Kathy, by her own admission, was not interested in any Philosophy course, but it was the only thing she could take to fill in her schedule. I on the other hand, was quite motivated and enjoyed class discussions, the assigned reading, etc. Kathy just wanted to

154

pass, nothing more, so she'd often go to the beach with some of the other girls to "study."

"Kath....you can't learn this stuff unless you're there."

"I don't have to understand it, just spit it back on a test, which I can do fine," she responded. And, that's how she looked at a lot of the "mandatory" courses, which were out of her major, elementary education. Frankly, she was a very good student and got good grades whether she liked a class or not.

"Well, I don't think you can pull this class off. Let me help you, okay?"

So, we discussed the differing perspectives of philosophy throughout history as relating to the Bible (sounds a bit boring, I know!). Of course, to do so, I'd often join her at Beverly Beach, a small, sandy little cove a couple of miles away from the school. Many students would hang out this time of year. The result? I couldn't believe it, but she got a B and I got a C! At few days later, we headed for the beach to study...well, to swim, get some sun and *perhaps* at least *talk* about studying.

"How did you get a B?" I asked her in utter disbelief.

"I just memorized the stuff you told me to look for and gave it back, that's all, *unless, of course, you feel I'm just more intelligent?*" She looked at me and smiled mischievously.

At that point, I was going nowhere, *given I had no immediate proof to the contrary!* "I'm going for a swim," I moaned, and I dove into the cool frothy waters, hoping to stimulate my intellectual capacities.

Then, there was a Psych class in which I practiced Kathy's philosophy of getting a good grade. The class was entitled, "Psychological Statistics," which at the time was being taught by a new, Asian professor, who spoke very limited English. He was hired, as many colleges do, to attract financial support because of a person's career reputation or accomplishments, not because of his or her teaching ability. Well, this man, as smart and educated as he was, was a student's nightmare. Few could understand him, and a lot of complaints were sent up line, though nothing changed. We only had one exam for our grade (it was a pass/fail course) and I, along with quite a few others, were definitely out in the cold as having any idea of how to decipher his lectures in real time.

So, I went to the best kid in the class and said, "Hey...I'm sunk, here. I'm only marginal in math anyway, and statistics...well, can you help me?"

He said, "Ed, just look for these words and then plug in the proper formula I'm giving you...you'll pass, don't worry. Forget trying to understanding it all...just apply the formula." So, I did as he instructed me to do and...unbelievably...I passed!

The last story I have is something I did in taking a final exam that I figured would get me a higher grade. Now...*I don't recommend this at all*...I'm just sharing what happened, okay?

It was a multiple-choice, history final exam, and I knew I might struggle just to get a C, for that was the results I had had in it throughout the semester thus far. So, I went through all the answers out of 100 questions and selected those that I knew for sure were correct. Next, I went through all the remaining, unanswered questions and made my best choice. Okay, now, assuming that I'm probably going to get a C anyway, this would mean that 25% of these "unsure" questions, which I had just answered, would be wrong...right? So, I went back and identified 25% of the *most* unsure, and changed my answer to my second choice, assuming it would probably be right by default.

Right now, perhaps you're thinking I'm a good case study for that very psych statistics class, or, that I should be psychoanalyzed. But, I want you to know that it worked. Of course, that's assuming that 25% of everyone else's scores were...well...never mind. If you're in high school or college...*just study hard, okay!*

Life Lessons

One of the lessons we all learned in the cabin and home-building years was to never count on anything to *work perfectly*. No matter how hard you tried, there was always a leak in the roof *somewhere!* And, if you didn't keep the cabin door perfectly shut, some critter would come in and try to build a nest under your bunk.

In other words, practically speaking, one thing always proves true...something will always come up to challenge our efforts at living a successful and well-prepared life. Life happens!

Seriously, life *can* be annoying at times, right? This or that didn't work out the way you expected or the timing of it ruined your plans. As I mentioned before, "Murphy's law" seems to be written in stone (the unexpected always happens). In the end, only God knows what we will face up ahead in our lives.

So, how can we make plans, yet move forward with hope...even if it's just a little hope that things will work out as desired? Well, Romans 8:28 does give us hope, of course, knowing God is working in all things for good. But, I'm thinking more about *how we should face* issues, problems, deflated expectations, failure, annoyances and just plain bothersome consequences.

I'd like to suggest that God expects us to work at having *patient trust* in his *overriding* purposes for our lives. Often, when things "go wrong," or when our plans fall apart, it may not be so bad, frankly, *if we allow such things to teach us.* Such things may be something God *purposefully* places into our experience for growth reasons, or to prepare us for some project or life calling later on.

My advice is this...all of us need to *own and accept life as it comes to us.* Let God challenge you, build you (even annoy you!) as he sees fit, while you do the best to follow his lead in humble faith. Practice this: *"Trust in the Lord...and do not lean on your own understanding."* Remember, statistically speaking, it's been shown that probably 25% of your life choices will be right, while 75% of your choices will....oh, never mind!

Roommates

As a teenager, the word roommates meant a bunch of guys you bunked with in a cabin at camp. I always enjoyed those winter and summer retreats, staying up late, eating chips and drinking soda, while talking  into the wee hours of the morning. If you wanted to room with someone, your youth director would usually accommodate you. But, in college one usually doesn't have a choice.

My first roommate at Houghton was a blond-haired, Florida-raised guy by the name of Jeff. Now, I was from Connecticut and folks from different ethnic or racial backgrounds didn't really phase me much. But, Jeff had a different slant on things.

"Look, they're not bad people. But, we live separately, that's all."

"Okay, but I'm asking why. In other words, how come blacks and whites live separately down there? What about in churches?"

"All the church people are the same way, mostly," he responded. "We try to just let everyone do their own thing…you know, on their side of street," Jeff returned.

Each time Jeff and I shared with each other about racial politics, he was very consistent. "This is the way we get along and it works fine," he would say. Of course, he probably didn't know very much about those other folks, because he didn't care to get to know them in the first place. If he had, and if more churches in that day would have done so too, racial equality would have come along much faster in our country.

Frankly, it really never occurred to me to look down on someone, because of their color or heritage. In New England our church and its youth group was mixed, and the kids always got along fine. And, my parents were open and tolerant people as well. How about you and your upbringing?

When returning to Gordon College, I did get the opportunity to choose my roommate. His name was Richard, and he was a couple of years older than I and a new believer from our home church. Richard was a great guy and a very sincere individual. He had been abused as a younger guy and had some issues relating to that. But, he genuinely came to Christ with his whole heart. He was sort of a quiet and a "to himself" type of guy, not given to having a lot of friendships. Our differences didn't separate us, though, because of our mutual love for Christ.

I've got to tell you about one prank a couple of the dorm guys and I played on him. Richard tended to sleep a lot, and when he would wake up, he'd sort of be in "la-la land," you know, groggy and confused for a minute or so. Well, one day he came back to the room about 4 o'clock in the afternoon on a day when darkness came at around 7:00 PM. He was sweaty and tired, after playing soccer, and he just collapsed on his bed.

"Ed…wake me up at 6 pm, okay, so I can shower and get outa here. I've got a special class tonight and *can't* miss it. Man…am I tired," and he fell sound asleep.

A bunch of us had been waiting for the opportunity, so I ran out, got them and then started our prank. We spray-painted the windows in our dorm room black, lightly enough, however, to see through so as to appear like it was genuine night time; we then set Richard's clock to 7:30 pm. But, we also set the alarm to go off in *three minutes.* I undressed and jumped into my bunk, so that when the alarm went off, Richard would awaken, thinking it was night

159

time and had missed his important class. The other guys would also be in their pajamas, but standing in the hall to make the thing look extra-real. Three minutes went by and....

"Ring!" The alarm went off on Richard's clock at the fake time of 7:30 PM (remember, it was really only about 6:00 PM and fully light outside). Richard let it ring several times, but finally stirred and then sat up on his bed, rubbed his head and tried to awaken himself. Suddenly, he glanced at the clock again and realized that he was a half hour late! He jumped up, looked out the window and thought it was now night and dark outside.

He looked at me fake-sleeping in bed, and shouted, "Oh no...I over-slept!" Ed, why didn't you get me up?" He started running and tripping over things in the room. He grabbed a couple of things, ran out the door and down the hall to the shower. The guys in the hall couldn't contain themselves, and started laughing their heads off, which immediately got his attention.

"What's goin' on?" he asked, groggily, and they explained the prank we had played on him. He was always a good-natured guy, so he laughed along with us. He never tried to get us back, but the confusion and consternation showing in his face when he started running around crazy-like, was something to behold.

Life Lessons

All of us are roommates in a giant dorm called life. Some get along well with everyone, some don't get along with others at all. And, of course, there are all kinds of folks in between.

In the church, that dorm space gets smaller, and in the family, it really gets tight, doesn't it! In the church family and at home, it's often difficult to live with differences. Such differences can just annoy us or even separate us. And, when you throw in differing cultures, well, that brings in a whole new set of variables, right?

Smaller differences aside, God tells us to love one another, whether you prefer someone better than another, or if you dislike someone else. Short-cut black hair, or long, purple-colored hair...

rings on your fingers or rings in your nose…it doesn't matter as far as kindness goes. Handsome or not, well-dressed or not, well-spoken or not, rich or poor, educated or not, high-tech or low-tech…all of us need to be kind and compassionate to one another. We should even be loving to our enemies, as well as to those that mistreat us!

From God's point of view, loving-kindness simply has no color or culture attached to it, for we're pretty much cut from the same cloth, despite personality flavors and various cultural odds and ends.

Why do people hate, dislike, favor or hold themselves above others so easily? The Bible says that it's because of our self-centered and sinful attitudes…and, it's even found in the church.

> *"My brothers, as believers in our glorious Lord Jesus Christ, don't show favoritism…If you show special attention…have you not discriminated among yourselves and become judges with evil thoughts?"* (James 2:1-4 NIV)

The problem with differences, though, is that *some* differences are not morally or Biblically acceptable. So, while God asks us to be kind and loving to everyone, he is not asking us to become intimate friends with everyone, or to participate with them in sinful or unwise behaviors. *In fact, he wants us to stay a safe distance away from anyone whose lifestyle is not compatible with our spiritual values* (check out II Cor. 6:14-18). Now, we do have to attend school, work alongside or have general social contact with all kinds of people from differing backgrounds and moral values. But, having close and intimate relationships with everyone isn't wise and it's not Biblical. Friendliness, always, but in friendship be cautious. As believers, *we aren't better than anyone else, we're just forgiven.* But, God asks us to maintain a godly lifestyle, which can be drastically upset, if we choose unwise relationships.

Whatever happened to my friend, Richard? Not sure, but I do know he never took a nap before class again!

The Blizzard

"Good to see you guys," I said, as I greeted two of my friends from the Cheshire Teens, who were up for the weekend to visit me and Kathy.

"Yeah....we got here just in time. They're calling for some snow...hopefully not too much," responded Tim. Tim and his brother, Rocky, were leaders in my home youth group and were considering attending Gordon sometime in the future. It was awesome to have some friends from home to catch up on all the "gossip" about the group. Previous to attending college, Kathy and I were teen leaders in the same youth group. Sometimes we would call Al, the church's Youth Director, in the middle of their Saturday night outreach meeting, before the group of 80 -100 teenagers hit the road for bowling, miniature golf, etc. The group loved hearing from us on the loud speaker, and we so enjoyed talking with them, as well.

"Okay," I said to Tim, "what do you want to do first." I began by showing the guys around the campus, then we all went to the cafeteria for supper. Looking outside, the snow was beginning to come down, though it was fairly normal to get a couple of inches or so this time of year. So, we really didn't suspect anything out of the ordinary.

After dinner, however, we knew something was up. The wind had picked up significantly, and there were already a couple of inches of the white stuff on the ground. We went to the rec hall, played some pool and then made it over to the lounge to watch some TV. By the time we left, there were several inches of snow on the ground, and it was coming down almost laterally, even sticking to the windows. It was also getting colder, so we went back to the dorm for cover. My roommate and I had our own bunks, of course, but we laid out the guys' sleeping bags on the floor. We had big plans in the morning to take them for an area tour to some local mansions, even taking the "T" to downtown Boston. We talked for an hour or so, then fell off to sleep.

The next morning, I awoke earlier than usual and stumbled over to a window, which overlooked the campus from our dorm. "You've got to be kidding. Look at this!" I exclaimed.

The guys stirred themselves awake and made their way slowly to the window to see what was up. They may have been half asleep themselves, but what they saw woke them up fast. There was well over a foot of fresh fallen snow on the ground...and it was still snowing and blowing!

Well, that changed all plans for the day, because no one was even allowed on the roads. Frankly, all of us had a great time that day wading through the snow, building forts and having snow-ball wars. Back in the dorm later on, we recorded a crazy, made-up story for the fun of it, acting out some wild parts and creating some wacky sound effects. We called it: "Tarzan, the Magnificent." (I still have that tape today).

Everyone on campus was just stuck there for the day, while the snow kept coming down. The Boston stations were going crazy with their warnings to stay home, saying there was more on the way. By the time the storm finally ended....two days later...we had about 5 feet of drifting snow on the ground! Student cars in the parking lot were literally *covered over*, and most of the dorm windows were plastered on the outside with caked-on snow.

The guys eventually returned home with a ton of fun experiences, as they survived the worst blizzard in the area for a decade. After they left, I remember having a couple of wintery walks along Manchester's rural roads with Kathy. The snow was plowed so high on each side, you could barely see beyond the mounds. But, when you did, you saw those covered fields of snow sparkling in the sunlight against a deep blue sky. Again, God's handiwork was always gorgeous and awesome!

Life Lessons

Are you a good "planner?" I mean, can you look ahead and prepare yourself for either what you know is coming or what may come unexpectedly? I'm about average, I guess.

However, some things do require good foresight in order to avoid unnecessary problems. As I'm writing this, the Western New York area is being blitzed by a huge, week long snow storm that's dumped over 7 feet of snow a few miles to the south of where I live. The thruway has been closed for four days, side roads left impassable and cars literally buried all over. Everyone is asking questions like: "Were our officials prepared for this? Did they plan properly for such an event?

Snow storms come and go. But, death is the ultimate snow storm, and many are not prepared for it. Will you be spending eternity with God and his Son, Jesus Christ? Choosing to trust in Christ as one's Savior and Lord is a life altering and eternity changing decision. The Bible says, *"He that has the son has life; he who does not have the Son of God does not have life."* (I John 5:12 NIV)

Perhaps you do know Christ as your Savior and Lord. Okay, here's another important question, "Are you adding to your spiritual foundation things that please God and impact eternity?"

> *"If any man's works which he has built on it remains, he will receive a reward. If any man's work is burned up, he will suffer loss..."* (I Cor. 3: 15)

Have you been a wise builder? (snow forts don't count!)

"It's The Truth!"

When I went to Gordon, all the great memories of my Cheshire Youth Group led me to seek out a youth sponsor position at a local church. I was a good relationship

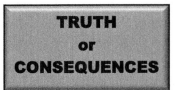

builder and fairly creative in designing attractive events for high school age kids. We'd have Wild Goose Chases, Splash Parties, Ghost Walks, Scavenger Hunts, Band Nights, etc., as well as your typical summer camps and winter retreats. I found a church that wanted an aggressive youth program, engaged the help of several other students from the college and began. The Pastor was very supportive, and soon we were able to get a fairly large number of teens to attend our Saturday night outreach events. During the week, I'd run Bible studies in homes or in the schools around my course schedule.

....

"We're off," I shouted to the kids in the bus. Our driver pulled the yellow school bus away from the front of the church, while everyone sang a couple of favorite choruses. The bus was full of excited teenagers on their way to the beach on this hot, sunny day in July. It took over eight hours to get where we were going, but we arrived on schedule. We traveled to a local church, which I knew well, and where we could simply throw our sleeping bags on the gymnasium floor for the night.

About an hour after we arrived, we headed over to the beach. Everyone got into the scene...some swimming, others throwing footballs and still others just sitting around eating! However, I soon noticed that one of the teenage guys, who I'll call Ted, was on the far end of the beach, talking with another person, whom I didn't recognize. I let it pass for the time being, and the rest of the day went great....lots of fun and plenty of food.

The next morning at the church found us reviewing our schedule for the day. Suddenly, a teenager came running down the hall shouting, "Ed, come quickly, Ted cut his hand real bad!" So, we both ran back down the hall to where the incident happened. Ted was holding his hand up, because it was bleeding quite a bit. The door window behind him was smashed, and we quickly realized what had happened. There had been a disagreement, some pushing around and then Ted smashed the window, though he only intended to vent his frustration, not to actually hit anyone.

As we attended to his bleeding hand in the nearby men's room, I thought about the whole context. One doesn't put his hand through a door window in anger like that, and Ted wasn't given to such anger, anyway, as a rule. So, what was up?

After questioning everyone, and then recalling the meeting Ted had with the unknown person at the beach, we became aware that Ted had purchased some drugs. He was a bit "high," and the anger he felt in his discussion with the other teen at the church just sent him over the top. Now, please understand that *Ted acknowledged none of this.* He maintained his innocence like a seasoned politician, even adding tears and pleas of mercy! Nevertheless, it was later proven true, so I needed to send him home alone on a commercial bus later that day.

After we had all returned home, I visited his house and discussed the whole event with his parents, who really came down on him. But, even then, he would not "fess-up" to the situation, instead pleading passionately that his explanation "was the truth!"

Life Lessons

Lying comes so easy, doesn't it, and truth is so difficult at times to face up to. So, we bend it, stretch it, manipulate it and cover it up like a dog hiding its bone in the ground. If it serves us well, we may even broadcast our lies loudly to gain followers; but if not, we just disperse it to fit our needs of the moment. Jesus said:

> *"...I am the Way and the Truth and the Life; no one comes to the Father except through Me."* (John 14:6)

To know Jesus is to live our lives truthfully, honestly and forthrightly...it's just part of the deal, you might say. Believers must live out their lives knowing that God expects them to resist the urge to lie or to be dishonest. Proverbs 12:22 says: *"The Lord detests lying lips, but he delights in men who are truthful."* Is it not better, then, despite the consequences, to practice the truth? Nevertheless, sometimes, people even lie to themselves:

- Like the young thief who tells himself that it was okay to steal a guy's watch because he "deserved it!" Translation: he's a mean kid, anyway, and no one likes him. So it's alright to steal from him.
- Like the girl working in the restaurant, who takes $40 out of her fellow waitress's purse in the back room. "She's got a lot of money anyway...her parents can buy her anything she wants!" Translation: She's rich and I'm not. Let's even things up a bit...she'll never miss it anyway.

And, of course, most times people lie just to avoid getting caught. Ask yourself if you would be willing to tell the truth, even if in so doing, you would be on the receiving end of either shame or punishment. That's the type of integrity God desires for all of us to possess. When it's modeled, it draws genuine appreciation and causes people to believe in the Savior you're telling them about.

Lying, on the other hand, is like putting hot sauce on ice cream. It's out of character and ruins the taste. Think about that the next time you must choose to either *"face it or fake it."* It *also* helps, when you're at the beach, that you enjoy the sand and surf instead of making friends with temptation.

"Beautiful, But Broken"

"This is so beautiful. I'm glad we came, aren't you, Ed?" Kathy and I were walking, mostly climbing, along the ragged rocks off Marblehead's shoreline.

"Yeah, but, we better not stay too long. This storm is supposed to hit pretty soon. I don't want to get wet and...."

A huge wave crashed on the boulder in front of me along the water's edge, sending foamy spray all over us. Kathy stepped back, and I barely kept my footing on a mossy rock. I regained my balance and stepped upon a boulder a bit farther away from the crashing surf.

"This may be beautiful, Kath, but these waves aren't anything to fool around with."

"I know...I know....but, look at the size of those over there."

She pointed to a spot just around the corner, where the full force of the surf was breaking onto the rocky shoreline. These were large boulders, some of them the size of a small car. They were stacked along the shoreline forming a 30' wide barrier in order to keep the surf from eroding the road. The local roads here were only the size of a driveway in width and meandered lazily along Marblehead's rugged shore line and its 15 mph speed limit.

Marblehead was a small, Massachusetts community near Manchester about 10 miles from the college. Again, the roads along the ocean's edge were narrow, sandy and bordered by quaint little houses and shops. It was a tiny little town, home to those who just wanted to enjoy a quiet, retirement setting. The picturesque harbor was filled with smaller sized boats tied to the dock. A few yachts were anchored in a nearby harbor, resting in the safety of those normally quiet waters.

As we walked along the slippery boulders, the waves began coming in faster, and the wind was beginning to howl. Salt spray kept blowing in our faces and our feet became soaked in the surging waters as they washed over the rocks. It seemed best to leave the rocks, so we climbed back up to our car, which was parked along the roadside.

Once inside the car, we peered through the windshield, while the rain pinged heavily on the glass. In just a few minutes, it seemed, giant waves started splashing 10 feet high along the boulders at the water's edge. Even the car itself was beginning to shift slightly in the strong winds, so we decided to turn around and head back to the college for safety. We wanted to beat the storm before it came to shore in full force, and I was glad we did.

Life Lessons

Did you know that there are over 117 million lakes in the world and 100 mountains rising to over 23,000 feet? Were you also aware that the deepest point in the ocean is located in the Mariana Trench east of the Philippines and is known as the Challenger Deep? (about seven miles down). You could actually submerge Mt. Everest into it. Did you know that there are over 230,000 species of fish in the seas, and over 10,000 kinds of birds, with a world-wide population between 200 to 400 billion. And, were you also aware that there are over 100 billion galaxies in the universe with over 100 billion stars in each one? (give or take a few billion, of course!) Yes, when God created the heavens and the earth, his awesome power certainly earned Him the name "Master Designer of the Universe."

Unfortunately, however, our world is also infected with a fallen condition known as sin, which has spoiled its glory to some degree. First, it is no longer free from *decay and death*...trees die, grass withers, and lakes become polluted and destroyed by overgrown algae. Second, it can become *dangerous* and out of control, hence the tremendously destructive power of hurricanes, earthquakes, floods and tsunamis. The waves of the 2011 Japan tsunami inundated more than 500 square kilometers of land, destroyed and/or damaged over 375,000 buildings, washed away over 240,000 cars and, sadly, killed as many as 15 to 20 thousand people. Third, our world will eventually be "updated" by God sometime in the future, and a "new heaven and earth" will be brought into existence sometime after Christ's return.

Here's my point. God created this gorgeous world of color and beauty, so we have every reason to enjoy it. However, let's remember that this world is not our eternal home, for God has something even better for those who know him as their personal Savior and Lord. With that in mind, let's avoid being complacent about what's most important...our relationship with Christ. Work, family, sports, vacations, travel, education, recreation... though important...should never become our life priority. We live because God gave us breath to live. And, He's got a whole, big universe for us to explore and enjoy...so keep your eyes on Jesus!

> *"Do not love the world or anything in the world. If anyone loves the world, the love of the Father is not in him. For everything in the world – the cravings of sinful man, the lust of his eyes and the boasting of what he has and does – comes not from the Father but from the world. The world and its desires pass away, but the man who does the will of God lives forever."* (I John 2:15-17 NIV)

Mr. and Mrs. Salty

It was good to be back at college, and especially to have Kathy there, too, who transferred there one semester before me.

Manchester By The Sea

As I said, Gordon College is located about 20 miles north of Boston, Massachusetts, in the area commonly called the North Shore. It is a wooded landscape, which hosts many small towns throughout, such as Marblehead, Rockport and Manchester. Boston itself boasts of a rich New England heritage of early American history, including familiar towns such as Lexington and Concord. There is a "T" (subway) that traveled from Boston to within a couple of miles from Gordon, and college kids often took it to go to downtown to see the Celtics play, visit the Philharmonic or just walk the famous "Freedom Trail."

However, during college, Kathy and I both needed money to help pay expenses, as well as for "fun" money, too. So, she took a job as a part-time governess for a wealthy area family I'll refer to as the Salty's, who lived in Manchester, Mass. I took a part-time job as an estate grounds-keeper for another family in the area. Kathy's family had three children, and she helped out with transporting the kids here and there, cooking and general housekeeping. Mr. Salty was greatly involved with Boston politics and Mrs. Salty was devoted to her family and involved in some community causes. Because I knew Kathy, I often visited her, while she worked at the Salty's home.

Over the next three years, Kathy and I became very close to Mr. and Mrs. Salty. We were just two displaced kids from Connecticut, who knew very few people in the area and who missed being away from home. But, the Salty's "took us in" as part of their family, and we became dear friends over the years.

. . . .

"Ed, be sure not to flush the toilet, okay?" shouted Mr. Salty from *outside* as he dug into the ground to unplug the septic system. He was a handyman type guy and enjoyed getting away from the office and Boston politics to work on his house. The Salty's had a beautiful, sixteen room home in Manchester with a luscious, well-manicured lawn and a gorgeous ocean front setting.

"No problem, Mr. Salty," I responded....and then, without thinking, routinely pushed down the handle, which flushed the toilet.

"Oh, no!" I mumbled to myself and counted the seconds for Mr. Salty's reply.

"Hey, what the....." Mr. Salty was really upset. "Ed, what did I tell you! Didn't you hear me!?"

Well, the whole system and all that sludge just backed up on him...and I mean all over him. How could I have been so dumb! Mrs. Salty intervened and calmed him down. Later on, we all laughed about why we didn't take a picture of him standing there, covered head to foot with dark, unmentionable sludge and just exasperated at my brainless act.

Life Lessons

Two things emerge from this particular experience. First, it's great to have friends who really care for you. The sense of family warmth and support the Salty's shared with us over the years was simply wonderful. They even offered to help pay for my graduate school costs, which was a great blessing in and of itself. And, the fun both Kathy and I had with their kids, transporting them here and there and doing things around the house, was a special pleasure as well.

Secondly, it's also great to have people around you who can *forgive* you when you do "stupid" things, like forgetting something important as not flushing a toilet! Seriously, good friends are like that. The pot holes and relational bumps in the road smooth out quickly in light of the fondness each has for the other.

On the other hand, a word should also be said about being responsible, too, especially about following through with others' expectations of you. It only takes a few mishaps to define your character to others, and that can type-cast you quickly. If you are reliable and responsible in all areas of your life, people will respect you and speak honorably about you. But, if you continue to be somewhat foolish, empty-headed or unreliable, that reputation will come back to bite you as well.

That's how it is with God, too, by the way. Our heavenly Father wants us to make wise choices and gives us more freedom and blessing as we show him that we can be trusted. It's not "rocket science," just the law of accountability, which he asks us to respect and keep.

How can you become more trustworthy, reliable and dependable? Well, always try to "think things through thoroughly." Repeat to yourself what is asked of you, ask for further information and write things down, if you have to. With some folks, just *slowing down* helps immensely, instead of being in such a rush to do whatever is asked of you. Also, take the time to *mentally process important things so that you fully understand what is required of you,* and make your efforts a matter of ongoing prayer as well. All this may help you to avoid pushing down on a handle that only drudges up a lot of nasty consequences.

"You who are simple, gain prudence; you who are foolish, gain understanding." (Proverbs 8:5 NIV)

The Gift

The Salty's lived along the Manchester shoreline, as I mentioned, and probably owned about 10 acres of land adjacent to the ocean, which was very wooded and hilly.

The house itself sat on a large, grassy lot sort of carved out of a cliff-like overhang at the edge of the woods.

Mrs. Salty liked to climb up that 50' overhang, sit relaxingly on the ground and overlook the ocean. One day I thought it a good idea to build her a little wooden chair up there, instead of her having to sit on the ground with all the bugs, ants and whatever else liked to scurry around her up there. So, I asked permission to do so, and she gladly approved of my endeavor. I began the project on a Saturday, and it only took about a couple of hours.

To begin, I scrounged around the estate for a while, digging up some old wood, a hammer, nails, etc. Then, I saw a sturdy log in the woods that seemed perfect as a base for the chair, so I dragged it over and started to work on it. When finished, it didn't look like anything one would want to buy, but I shared the finished product with Mrs. Salty, who was quite pleased.

As I was putting on the final touches, however, I stepped over to a spot deeper into the woods behind the chair and its perch. I was clearing the pathway leading up to top, making sure it wasn't too rocky or slippery. Actually, that path crossed the back lawn of the house, went into the brush along its base and then wound upwards through brush and small trees to Mrs. Salty's spot. For a second, I lost my footing, but dug my heel into the soft, mossy dirt alongside of it to steady myself. Looking down, I spotted a couple of bees emerging from the grass, so I moved away. In no time, there were ten bees buzzing around me, then twenty, then thirty! I recognized that I had unfortunately stepped into a buried yellow-jacket nest! I quickly ran down the pathway, confident that I had avoided a painful encounter and kept walking toward the house.

Suddenly, I screeched, "Ouch!" as I felt a bee sting me in my groin area. "Ouch...what's going on!" A second sting...same spot! My immediate reaction was to start running toward the back door and the kitchen area of the house. Mrs. Salty and another worker were looking out the open door and saw me running toward them full tilt across the back yard with arms waving in the air. I ran into the kitchen, kicking my legs wildly and grabbing my jeans to squelch these embedded creatures, when another one got me.

"Ouch! Man, that does it!" I shouted. I unbuckled my belt and ripped off my jeans, dancing a jig in my underwear in the presence of everyone, who thought I was crazy, of course.

"What are you doing, Ed!" Mrs. Salty yelled.

"Confounded bees....they're in my pants...I can't get rid of the darn things!" was my response, as I continued to swat the air around me for any bees that had followed me down the hill. I took the jeans and shook them up and down to rid them of any of those little yellow invaders. But, I didn't see any more.

"Jeepers, Ed," someone laughingly said, "maybe they're in your underwear?"

At that point, I realized this was not the most appropriate time to continue searching for bees, so I ran to the bathroom and stripped down. There I found a couple of yellow and black culprits and decisively ended their existence. In all my time at the Cabin in Cheshire, I don't think I was ever stung by bees, even when I blew up a nest in the back wall. Those stings really hurt, though they probably weren't as bothersome as the embarrassment I felt when returning to Mrs. Salty and her maid. Gosh!

Life Lessons

Life sometimes intimidates us a bit with uncomfortable events, and we simply walk away somewhat wiser. But, at other times it just "hits us where we hurt" the most. This event was a real "pain in the britches," and I remembered it for a long time thereafter. Consequences can certainly hurt, when they catch up with you.

Now, it wasn't that I had done anything wrong, frankly, just that I had not been careful enough. Anyone walking in the woods knows there are all kinds of potential threats one may encounter at ground level, especially bees. There are covered-up holes, snakes in rock crevices, easily annoyed critters like skunks, and all kinds of "bugs & slugs" to spoil your day. So, while working in the woods, one has to be especially ready for these situations, which means *watching where you walk.*

Consequences can hurt, whether they come by way of ill-chosen attitudes and actions, or simply by way of not thinking something through. I have a friend who would point to his head, slightly tapping it three times, when trying to get a point home to his son for his misbehavior. It meant, "You just didn't think, did you!"

One of the best ways to avoid mistakes in anything is to *consider the consequences first.* When NASA designed the shuttle, it had back-up systems for every imaginable contingency. They didn't want the consequences of a single, failed oxygen tank, for instance, to kill its crew.

Are you considering the *spiritual* consequences your present attitudes and actions might bring to you this week? Are you watching where you're walking, spiritually speaking? Remember, following God's will brings blessing, but, disobedience brings loss.

> *"Those who cling to worthless idols forfeit the grace that could be theirs."* (Jonah 2:8 NIV)

Life and Death

"So, that's how Joe Worm solved the 'Mystery of the Riverside Robberies.'"

"That was great...can I have another one?" asked Abbigail, the six year old daughter of Mr. and Mrs. Salty. At bedtime for the kids, I'd often create these adventure stories and tell them to Abby, followed by prayer. She just loved them. The main character was Joe Worm, self-appointed detective, solving mysteries around the town dump, where he lived. His helpful tribe of area characters included Blackie the Crow, Sir Bogglesworth, the local Great Dane of a nearby estate, and Sam Squirrel, a high energy powerhouse of local gossip. Joe would often climb onto Blackie's neck feathers and travel to nearby towns to hunt down malicious characters. At other times, forest dwellers, who were endangering the nearby swamp with evil intentions, would be foiled by Joe's heroic intervention (you can see I really get into these stories, right?).

"Abby...sorry, but it's time for lights out. Of course, let's pray first, okay?" Then, Abby would pray a few short prayers, and I would pray after her. I hoped that in the future, I could spark her interest in finding out more about Jesus and her need to come to him in saving faith. She attended a nearby church with her parents, which was very active in community care and good deeds. But, to my knowledge, I don't think that Abby ever made a personal commitment to Jesus Christ later on in her life. She was such a wonderful little girl, and I hope that one day I will find out that she has become a believer.

Abby had two siblings, an older brother and a sister. Her brother eventually became a successful lawyer, but her sister was unfortunately killed, while biking along the highway to their Cape Cod summer home. It was devastating to the family, as one  would suspect. *Why would God take a beautiful, young girl like this in such a horrific way and bring sadness to people, who were basically good and kind?*

I didn't try to explain it, for I really couldn't. I had some traditional answers I had learned in my youth group and at Christian college. But, when it hurts so deep inside, is there ever anything that really sooths the pain clawing inside your heart, when the unthinkable actually happens? We know that God is never the author of evil, but it is difficult sometimes to understand the "whys" of life, isn't it.

Time does heal, of course, but it heals slowly in many cases. Mr. and Mrs. Salty's pain eventually found a place of peace, but such a loss still left a mark that will only be healed in heaven, I believe. Nevertheless, they continued to be supportive in so many ways to Kathy and me, and I'm forever grateful for their kind friendship over the years. Abby really enjoyed my simple Joe Worm stories, though probably not as much as I enjoyed telling them!

Life Lessons

There are some things about life and God that are simple enough for a child to understand. For instance, prayer was an easy vehicle for her to see that God loves us and wants us to draw near to Him at all times.

On the other side, however, there are more difficult events in life, like her sister's death, that we often cannot answer so clearly.

That's when we need to rely upon our faith in God, because our capacity to understand just seems hollow. Answers given seem nothing more than echoes of uncertainty. Have you ever been there?

I've found that in such moments, my friends and my church are very important to me. They help me to find a place of rest in my search for answers, instead of an ongoing struggle with no end in sight. Let someone else share your struggles with things as they occur, okay, and you'll find it much easier to move forward. Then, perhaps, down the line, you'll find the answers that eluded you. If not, you'll still have the support you'll need to carry you through the difficult times of your life. Here's a helpful truth I picked up along the way, "We don't live by explanation, but by faith."

As you face and endure your particular difficulties in life, apply this principle faithfully: *let God be God.* In the sometimes painful or discouraging times ahead, though you may not understand why things happen the way they do, you do know the One who does. Trust him always, okay, because as God, he incapable of making mistakes or forgetting to take care of our needs. No matter how life unfolds itself before your eyes, know that he is beyond any blame in anything you might see. We may not understand this in all circumstances, but, of course, he does live above all circumstances, doesn't He.

> *"Do not let your hearts be troubled. Trust in God, trust also in me."* (John 14:1 NIV)

The Movie Star

There she was, Liza Minnelli, crossing Main street right in front of me in Manchester, Massachusetts. The movie company was on location in our little, seaside town for the filming of the movie, "Tell Me That You Love Me Julie Moon." I was just coming through town on my way to the Salty's, when I spotted a small crowd next to the drug store, and all the roads were blocked off around it. I parked in the town's grocery store

Liza At Manchester Harbor

nearby and close to the town's small railroad station, then walked over to the scene. There really weren't a lot of "Hollywood people" there, just some camera people, a director, a few actors, perhaps some security personnel, too.

Main Street in Manchester was just a sleepy little place about the size of a football field, with only a few cars moving along at a snail's pace. Apparently, movie companies on a "shoot," as they call it, try to avoid attracting a lot of onlookers, as well as not advertising very much about when and where they'll be filming. Otherwise, large crowds tend to interfere with their ability to film the scene correctly.

When I got there, Miss Minnelli was talking with another actor across the street by the store's front door. No one seemed to be in a hurry to start filming, for everything in the scene had to set up just right…lighting, action sequence, camera angles, sound, etc.

After a short while, the actors took their places inside the closed doorway. When the Director said, "Go," a young man in front of one of the cameras placed a chalk board with the scene number and name on it, and said something like, "Scene Two, Take Three," which started the action. Then, Liza emerged from the door with the other actor, talked briefly, then crossed the street in front of me. End of scene. Everyone regrouped and it looked like they were going to spend some time discussing things, so I left and returned to the Salty's house to pick up Kathy. It was very interesting to see how slow and methodical filming a movie can be.

I've always been impressed with acting. In our youth group, we used to create skits every week, but, of course, they were just to get everyone to laugh..."pie-in-the-face" type stuff. I do remember a time, however, when I was picked as a volunteer character at a Walt Disney World attraction. Before each show a Disney stunt coordinator would pick five volunteers from the audience as they were waiting to enter. The attraction brought the audience onto a huge, mock set for filming a WWII PT boat encounter with a Japanese plane dropping bombs on it. The volunteers were covered from head to toe in rain gear. A bit later, in front of the audience, they took part in filming a short, 30 second movie with loud water cannons exploding all over the place and water being catapulted into the air to simulate real bombs. I was the one selected to be the captain of the PT boat, sitting behind the steering wheel on the bridge. Upon command, a huge 100 gallon deluge of water was released on me to simulate an ocean wave hitting after a bomb drop. I had a great time acting my part, but, sadly, no one asked me to join the Disney World cast!

Life Lessons

It's easy to get enamored with popular or powerful people. But, in the end, we're all just about the same. God wants us to act with consistency, no matter who we bump into. We should learn to appreciate a person's special abilities or talents, of course. But, our attitudes toward them should be the same as with anyone else. It's not someone else's *fame* that should motivate us; it should be God's *favor* that we find more deeply valuable, for it has eternal rewards. The Bible says:

> *"The world and its desires pass away, but the man who does the will of God lives forever."* (I John 2:17 NIV)

Our society is unnecessarily dazzled by famous and successful people. Just look at the many magazines at the check-out counter of your local grocery store. It's not so much what they've accomplished in their profession that's the problem, it's that too many folks think their viewpoints are all that trustworthy or even praiseworthy. Being successful actors or actresses is not any guarantee of intelligence, integrity or spiritual insight, it's just a job like any other occupation. So, avoid being overly impressed by anyone in any profession or station in life....*credentials don't guarantee credibility.*

Graduation Day

All the parents were mingling and rushing about, trying to get the best seat to see their daughters and sons graduate from college. As the large crowd mingled about, I lined up outside with about 300 other students ready to parade into the college gymnasium to receive our diplomas.

The day was beautiful and sunny, a perfect one for such an event, not a cloud in the sky. All of us were somewhat nervous, of course, as we stood and reviewed the order of events. When called, we were to march into the gym accompanied by the familiar graduation processional, "Pomp and Circumstance."

We were all given a 3x5 card with our name and some other info on it. As I talked with the person with whom I was to march alongside, I moved my hand up with the card to shade my eyes from the brightness of the sun.

"Ouch," I gasped. I had unfortunately jammed the corner of that little card into my eye. "Man…that hurt!"

I lowered my hand with the card, and my eye started watering like crazy. It wasn't wildly painful, but it was more than just the annoying feeling you get, for instance, when a bug flies into your eye. Each time I rolled my eye or turned to look at someone, it scraped that small cut on my eye's cornea. And, again, it kept watering to the point that I couldn't look anyone in the face without appearing to be crying. What was I to do now?

Suddenly, the music began and the line started moving into the gymnasium. I tried to keep one hand over the scratched eye, which slowed down the incessant tearing somewhat, but I felt embarrassed, thinking everyone was looking at me. The line was long and the entrance slow, but we finally found our seats up front.

"Great," I said to my friend sitting next to me. "Maybe this will stop, now that I'm sitting down." But, it didn't…not one bit. In fact, it started hurting more. That 3 hour event was really one of the most unpleasant times I've ever had in my entire life. My eye was closed, but I covered it with a handkerchief someone had given me. How I was able to walk across that stage remains a mystery. Everyone must have thought I was crying or emotionally touched at the whole event, including the Dean, who handed me the diploma!

After all the hoopla at the ceremony's end, my family and I eventually ended up meeting outside, where I explained my unfortunate situation. We went out for lunch and ended up discussing what to do, because the pain just wouldn't go away. Finally, I went to the emergency room at a nearby hospital for something to put on it for healing, as well as for stopping the pain. The attending intern gave me some eye drops to put in every couple of hours, which I did faithfully.

My parents eventually went home and I settled in for the night. But, after faithfully applying those eye drops all night, getting no sleep and still finding no relief, I called Mrs. Salty for help the next morning. She immediately said she would take me to her father, a well-known Boston eye surgeon. It was Sunday, and he was semi-retired, but he opened up his office just for us.

He looked at the medicine I was applying and exclaimed, "Why are you using this stuff? It will only open up your cut even more!" I had been applying the wrong medicine for over a day, thanks to the ignorance or mistake of that emergency room intern.

Life Lessons

Interruptions can be annoying and unwanted. My plans for this day certainly did not include having a painful graduation.

You've probably heard the sports related phrase, "When the going gets tough, the tough get going." Well, life can be looked at as a big football or baseball game at times, when undesirable things happen to us. Here are some difficult things we often face.

- A bad habit that won't go way
- A school thing that brings stress and difficulty
- A job thing that causes us to get angry
- A church thing that brings strong disagreement

These and other situations can make us feel really bad and question our relationship with God or His providential care over us. Why did this have to happen? Couldn't God have done it differently? We might even say, "I just want to give up, that's all."

Okay....you're certainly free to give up, walk away, lay back... whatever. But...ask yourself this: *"Where are you gonna to go?"* Hey, all of us get angry at ourselves, at others and even at God at times (however, measure your words carefully with God). But, the point is...where can a believer go? Peter answers this question, when he faced difficulty and responded rightly: *"Lord, to whom shall we go? You have the words of eternal life." (Jn. 6:68)*

For the true believer, there's only one way...and it's back to God first, then to move forward. So, review your struggles and past issues, confess whatever sins you need to confess, and restore your relationship with God. Then, you can step forward confidently and better prepared to be all God wants you to be.

To sum it up, all of us need to "tough it out" at times in our lives...to persevere and keep going in faith and obedience. That's the only way we can "graduate with honors" in whatever life education God brings upon us. Again, Peter reminds us:

> *"After you have suffered a little while, (God) will himself restore you and make you strong, firm and steadfast."*
> (I Peter 5:9-10 NIV)

A Look Backward and Forward

"I can hardly wait to see it," I said to Kathy, who was now my wife. Along with our two young children, Bobby and Kerri, we were on our way to visit her mother in Cheshire, just a few miles away from the Cabin Home. Of course, it wasn't a cabin any longer, but a large and beautiful home in the woods. Nevertheless, it had been many years since my eyes had seen it, and I was really excited to do so. We planned to go there first, and I hoped the owner wouldn't mind us just stopping by like this.

Once we got off the highway, we made our way up that long hill from Wallingford to Cheshire, winding around those country roads. Reaching our destination, I slowed the car to a crawl by the tree across from the driveway and made a right turn. The old spruce tree that stood to the right was no longer there, but there was a paved driveway now. And, there next to the driveway by the street was that large gully, now overgrown, where we dragged and burned all the cleaned-out brush and fallen tree limbs cluttering up the front of our property. As a young boy, I enjoyed watching the flames leap into the air, sometimes as much as ten feet.

As we inched up the driveway, I was recalling many of my childhood memories. There was the long archery range I had cleared out of the woods; though it was so overgrown one could barely make it out. The stream along the right side of the driveway was now very small, just trickling down through the weeds and dead leaves.

"Wait a minute," I exclaimed, startling the kids in the back seat. I think....yes, I think that's the huge spruce tree I used to climb. Gosh, it just looks so different." The woods were so overgrown, it was impossible to be certain.

186

"Hey, Bobby, wouldn't you like to climb that?" I asked. He didn't seem to have the same excitement that I did about it.

We came to the curve at the bottom of the large, sloping hill leading up to the cabin house. I laughed as I remember my friends and I sledding down that short, but steep hill, catapulting ourselves over the snow jump we used to make in the middle. Sliding the old car backwards along the deep, dirt tracks that once were there also grabbed my attention.

As we slowly crept up the hill, I felt a warm sense of "being home" that overwhelmed me, even though for years I'd been away and had my own home now. At the top I saw the circle of pines, where cars used to turn around. It was now gone and replaced by a large garage next to the house. I turned to the left and parked the car at the flat area at the top of the hill.

"Dad, it's so big," Bobby exclaimed.

"Do you think anyone will mind us being here, Dad?" asked Kerri as she looked around. "I mean, I don't see anyone…no cars or anything. Should we get out?"

"I think it's okay. If we need to, we can just explain we were former owners."

So, we all got out and started walking around. We walked along the front, and, seeing no furniture in the house, we assumed it was unoccupied (actually, the house was being sold. The owners had already moved away, as I found out later). The house had been painted, and a new addition on the far side had been added.

I stood on the front grass, while the kids ran around. I recalled how the dogs used to chase me through the snow to the tree fort in the back. And, there was that small stone wall along the front, which hid all the toads that would come out just before dark. I seemed to smell the camp fires the family enjoyed, which flickered in the night and popped noisy sparks into the darkness. At the edge of the front lawn, I looked down through the woods to the road, remembering how I hated raking all those fall leaves down that big embankment in front of the house.

I turned quickly to the right and looked across the driveway at the top of the hill to a spot about twenty feet into the brush. Was it still there?

"I've got to check it out," I mumbled, so I wandered over to the spot. Pushing through the undergrowth and brush, I stopped to look around, still searching, but unable to find what I was looking for.

"Where's that little cross," I whispered to myself, moving some leaves and scattered brush aside.

"Dad, what are you doing?" asked Bobby. He had seen me walking over here and ran over to check it out.

"Ah...well...Bobby, here's where I buried my very special dog...whose name was Dutchess. I loved her a lot. Just like you and Kerri love your dog, Ginger."

I turned and kept rummaging around for the two sticks I had tied together and placed on the mound, where I had buried Dutchess. Actually, I thought that perhaps I wasn't in the exact place, for everything...the driveway, the big old climbing spruce, the yard...everything seemed much smaller than I remembered it being. But, at that time I was much smaller, too, and my mind was having a hard time readjusting, I guess.

"Did you love her like we love Ginger, Dad?" asked Kerri, who by now had also wandered over.

"Yes, Kerri, very much so," I responded, as I my eyes got a bit watery. But, I caught myself and began to tell them about how much fun she had been and why I buried her here.

Soon, all of us returned to the car and left for our visit to Kathy's mother. We had a good visit for a day or so, and then returned to Buffalo, New York, where we currently lived. My visit had been full of childhood reminiscing, and I was happy to indulge myself in that wonderful time when we lived in the Cabin and afterwards in the home we built around it.

Life Lessons

Life changes quickly and with it go many fond memories of good times enjoyed with friends and family, mixed with some difficult times as well, of course. This visit brought both back into focus, but I was glad to revisit it all, as I'm doing with you in this second cabin book.

But, there's a funny thing about memories...one really can't fully recapture everything in the same way he or she experienced it. Memories are snapshots of times past, but those situations always change, sometimes greatly, sometimes just in small ways, but still remarkably different. The color of the lawn was darker and fuller now, the house more weather beaten, the woods more dense and familiar markers were moved or hard to find. Mr. Arthur had long passed away, and "Indian Rock" and those trails through the woods were incredibly smaller than I remembered them being. The ice skating pond was no longer there and the woods all around us were now sprinkled with newly built homes.

Perhaps this indicates the most important life question for all of us to ask ourselves: "Life changes, *but will we?*" There will always be good times and pleasant memories from our childhood and teenage years. But, such memories should do more than just stir our emotions; they should move us to thank God and love Him more faithfully.

The cabin and country home years provided me with more than just good memories. They give me godly principles to model and live by. Though God blessed me with them, it is up to me to enroot them into my heart so I can be all God wants me to be. How about you? Here's one of my favorite verses about times past, and I leave it with you to enjoy ...

189

Thus says the Lord: "Stand by the ways and see and ask for the ancient paths, Where the good way is and walk in it; And, you shall find rest for your souls...."
(Jeremiah 6:16)

Kathy and I

Have you ever dreamed of being a published author?

If you are interested,
GET STARTED TODAY by visiting
FreeChrisitianPublishing.com

CPSIA information can be obtained at www.ICGtesting.com
Printed in the USA
LVOW04s2131280915

456123LV00014B/197/P